Reading the Psalms Again for the First Time

Reading the Psalms Again for the First Time

A Spirituality for Justice-Seekers and Peacemakers

J. Clinton McCann, Jr.

CASCADE *Books* · Eugene, Oregon

READING THE PSALMS AGAIN FOR THE FIRST TIME
A Spirituality for Justice-Seekers and Peacemakers

Cascade Books
An Imprint of Wipf and Stock Publishers
199 W. 8th Ave., Suite 3
Eugene, OR 97401

www.wipfandstock.com

PAPERBACK ISBN: 979-8-3852-1151-7
HARDCOVER ISBN: 979-8-3852-1152-4
EBOOK ISBN: 979-8-3852-1153-1

Cataloguing-in-Publication data:

Names: McCann, J. Clinton, Jr., 1951– [author].

Title: Reading the Psalms again for the first time : a spirituality for justice-seekers and peacemakers / by J. Clinton McCann, Jr.

Description: Eugene, OR: Cascade Books, 2024 | Includes bibliographical references.

Identifiers: ISBN 979-8-3852-1151-7 (paperback) | ISBN 979-8-3852-1152-4 (hardcover) | ISBN 979-8-3852-1153-1 (ebook)

Subjects: LCSH: Bible.—Psalms—Theology. | Bible.—Psalms—Criticism, interpretation, etc. | Justice—Biblical teaching.

Classification: BS1430.5 M33 2024 (paperback) | BS1430.5 (ebook)

VERSION NUMBER 09/13/24

Dedicated to the faculty, students, staff, and Board of Directors of Eden Theological Seminary, past and present, with gratitude for the opportunity to teach, learn, and work with you all, and with appreciation for Eden Seminary's commitment to the pursuit of the justice, righteousness, and peace that God wills for the human family and for the whole creation.

Contents

Preface

THE FOLLOWING SUGGESTIONS AND remarks provide a brief orientation to the readers of this volume:

1. Because full translations of the psalms discussed are not provided, it will be helpful to have an English translation (or several English translations) close at hand. Unless otherwise noted, quotations from Scripture are from the New Revised Standard Version (NRSV). When other translations of the Bible are quoted or referred to, they will be identified as follows: The Common English Bible (CEB); the Jewish Publica tion Society (JPS); the Revised Standard Version (RSV); the New International Version (NIV). I frequently offer my own translations, which will be identified simply as "my translation." When citing the Psalms, I have used the English versification rather than the Hebrew.

2. I have not assumed that readers of this volume will know Hebrew, although I do occasionally include Hebrew words or phrases. They will appear in italics, and a translation will be provided.

3. I refer frequently to "the psalmist" or "the psalmists." While the name "David" appears with seventy-three psalms, this should not be taken as an indication of authorship. In fact, we

do not know who wrote the Psalms; and this is the rationale for referring simply to "the psalmist" or "the psalmists."

4. It has become increasingly evident in recent years that interpreters themselves affect the interpretation of biblical texts. Undoubtedly, my interpretation of the Psalms reflects in some measure my identity, background, and context. I am a university-trained biblical scholar and an ordained clergyperson who teaches at an ecumenical Protestant seminary. While I work in a Christian context and write from a Christian perspective, I aim fully to honor the origin of the Psalms in ancient Israel and Judah, as well as to acknowledge their transmission and use by Jews and Christians over many centuries. Thus, I hope that this volume will be of interest and use to persons of various identities and from diverse backgrounds and contexts—biblical scholars, pastors, rabbis, teachers, mission-planners, and others in the church and synagogue. And beyond Jewish and Christian circles, I dare to hope that people of other faiths or no faith at all may derive inspiration and instruction from the Psalms for the fashioning of a world in which all people (and the creation itself) are valued, attended to, and provided for—in short, a world of justice, righteousness, and *shalom.*

Acknowledgments

As every author knows, the writing, editing, and publishing of a book is a communal effort. So, there are many people to be thanked! I am grateful first of all to the Board of Directors and to my faculty colleagues at Eden Theological Seminary for the sabbatical leaves that afforded time for research, thinking, and writing. My faculty colleagues also discussed portions of the manuscript with me and offered helpful feedback and suggestions, as did several colleagues in the Society of Biblical Literature who were part of a study group called *Lemadim Olam* (Students Forever). In my experience, the real impetus for writing derives from the classroom; so I am very grateful to the many students of Eden Seminary, past and present, with whom I have had the opportunity to teach and learn about the Psalms, especially from the perspective of justice-seeking and peacemaking.

In my experience as well, the seminary classroom extends far beyond the campus; I am grateful for the opportunities I have had over the past several years to share and discuss the material of this book with numerous congregations and organizations, including the following in the St. Louis area (unless otherwise noted): Pilgrim UCC, Labadie, Missouri; Second Baptist Church; St. Timothy's Episcopal Church; Principia College, Elsah, Ilinois; First Presbyterian Church of Kirkwood; The Episcopal Church of the Good Shepherd; Gethsemane Lutheran Church; Emmanuel

Episcopal Church; Ladue Chapel Presbyterian Church; St. Lucas UCC; Sanibel Congregational UCC, Sanibel, Florida; University City United Methodist Church; the St. Louis Chapter of the American Guild of Organists; First Congregational Church, UCC, South Windsor, Connecticut; St. Charles Avenue Presbyterian Church, New Orleans (Lupburger Lecture Series); Holy Family Ecumenical Catholic Communion, Aurora, Colorado; Second Presbyterian Church's Men's Friday Morning Bible Study, Louisville, Kentucky; Hope UCC, DeSoto, Missouri; First Christian Church (DOC), California, Missouri; Westminster Presbyterian Church, Springfield, Illinois (Bay Weekend); Trinity Lutheran Church; Webster Groves Presbyterian Church; First Congregational UCC of Webster Groves (Practicing Our Faith group); Hope UCC; New Piasa Chautauqua, Chautauqua, Illinois; Columbia UCC, Columbia, Missouri; and Lutheran School of Theology, St. Louis.

And finally, many thanks to the Revd. Dr. Robin Parry, my editor, who kindly expressed an interest in publishing this volume and who has very helpfully guided me through the publication process. It has been a privilege to work with him and his colleagues at Cascade Books, an imprint of Wipf and Stock Publishers.

Introduction

"I Am for Peace" (Psalm 120:7)

"I AM FOR PEACE," the psalmist declares in the concluding line of Psalm 120. I take this affirmation to be a summary statement of the spirituality of the book of Psalms, and it is the purpose of this volume to tell you why I have reached this conclusion.

Spirituality is a popular topic these days, but the topic of spirituality is one of the most confusing in the whole area of religious and theological studies. Another layer of confusion is the fact that the term "spirituality" is used in fields that have nothing to with religion or theology. In one study of spirituality (by occupational therapists!), the authors identified no less than ninety-two distinct definitions of the term.[1] Almost all of these definitions focus on the human being—how people feel and what people think as well as what people do to construct meaning in their lives. This includes what people think about human existence and its purpose as well as what practices or disciplines people engage in to put themselves in touch with what they perceive to be the meaning of their lives or of human existence in general.

These person-centered definitions are valuable and helpful (see below), but in this volume I take a different approach. My starting point is God-centered rather than person-centered, and

---

1. Unruh et al., "Spirituality Unplugged," 5–19.

I shall focus on how the Psalms portray God and God's purposes for human existence and the life of the world. In short, I am interested primarily in what *God* thinks, feels, wills, and does, insofar as the Psalms have something to say about God. And they do! As James L. Mays points out, "The psalms . . . contain more direct statements about God than any other book in the two testaments of the Christian canon."[2]

So, in keeping with this explicitly theological approach, I risk proposing a ninety-third definition of spirituality that I have borrowed from my faculty colleagues at Eden Theological Seminary: "Spirituality is the work of God the Holy Spirit in our lives . . . calling us to the service of God's righteousness in the world."[3] What is God's work in the world? Our definition gives us a clue—that is, *righteousness* (see below). The Psalms are very explicit in reinforcing this direction, although we shall start with a different word that I take to be virtually synonymous—that is, *justice*. In a word, the will of God for the world, along with the work of God in the world, consists of justice. And the Psalms define justice as attention to and provision for the whole human community, especially those persons whose lives are most threatened and vulnerable—the impoverished, the weak, the needy, the oppressed. In fact, Psalm 82 (the keyword of which is *justice*) dares to define divinity or god-ness precisely in terms of a commitment to justice; and chapter 1 will focus on Psalm 82. Accordingly, as we shall see in chapter 2, the God of Israel is portrayed in Psalms 96 and 98 as having come into the world "to establish justice in the world with righteousness" (Pss 96:13; 98:9, my translation; see the CEB). As we shall see (and as already suggested above), justice and righteousness are virtually synonymous and frequently paired in the Psalms and elsewhere. Chapter 3 focuses on the earthly agents of God's will, especially the Judean kings, who were known as God's "son" (Ps 2:7), and whose job it was to do justice and righteousness, resulting in *shalom*—"peace" or "comprehensive well-being"—for the whole world (see Psalm 72).

2. Mays, *Preaching and Teaching*, 69–70.

3. Eden Theological Seminary Faculty, *Spirituality*, 3.

Subsequent chapters will consist of reading or re-reading several major types of psalms through the lens of God's commitment to justice, righteousness, and *shalom*—the *torah* psalms, especially Psalm 1 (chapter 4); the laments, which are also known as complaints, prayers for help, or protests (chapter 5); the imprecatory, cursing, or vengeance psalms (chapter 6); the hymns or songs of praise (chapter 7); the psalms of assurance, especially Psalm 23 (chapter 8); and the Songs of Zion (chapter 9). Chapter 10 will relate the book of Psalms to Jesus, suggesting not so much that we read the Psalms christologically but rather that we understand Christ "psalm-ologically." The conclusion, chapter 11, will return to Psalm 120 and its immediate neighbors, noting especially the emphasis on peace and justice in Psalm 122 and offering some concluding reflections on the spirituality of the Psalms.

Why This God-Centered Approach?

Several years ago, I was involved with several scholarly colleagues in a project that focused on how the Old Testament might faithfully and fruitfully be involved in Christian worship. My contribution to the volume was entitled, "The Hope of the Poor: The Psalms in Worship and Our Search for Justice."[4] One of my colleague's response to my essay was something like this: "I'm sure glad you wrote that essay, because my students have no idea that the Psalms might have anything to do with justice." My colleague's characterization of her students is probably a fair assessment of the opinion of most church folk (if they know anything at all about the Psalms)—that is, it would never occur to them that the Psalms might actually serve as an eloquent invitation to pursue God's justice, righteousness, and *shalom* in and for the world. One major purpose of this volume and its God-centered approach is to address this situation. For many people, it may be like reading the Psalms again for the first time, as the title of this volume suggests.[5]

4. McCann, "Hope of the Poor," 155–78.

5. As many will recognize, my title alludes to the work of Marcus Borg, *Meeting Jesus Again for the First Time*, which invited readers to understand

Perhaps the major reason for the failure to connect the Psalms with the pursuit of justice is what we suggested above—that is, the traditional approach to the Psalms and the spirituality derived from the Psalms has been person-centered. John Calvin, for instance, described the Psalms as an "'Anatomy of all the Parts of the Soul'; for there is not an emotion of which any one can be conscious that is not here represented as in a mirror."[6] And Martin Luther suggested that "everyone, in whatever situation he may be, finds in that situation Psalms and words that fit his case, that suit him as if they were put there just for his sake, so that he could not put it better himself, or find or wish for anything better."[7] Calvin and Luther were certainly on target! And their observations explain why the book of Psalms has been a devotional and spiritual classic for centuries—that is, faithful people have identified with the emotions and words of the psalmists, and the Psalms have given them words to describe their own experiences and feelings. John C. Endres, SJ, calls this an "'anthropo-centered' approach to psalms," and this approach has nurtured a pervasive and powerful form of spirituality.[8]

Let me be clear—it is not my intent to denigrate or diminish this approach to the Psalms or the type of spirituality that this approach has nurtured. The ability of the Psalms to function as Calvin, Luther, Endres, and Davis describe has been extraordinarily valuable and helpful, and I trust that it will remain so. My intent is, in essence, to extend the range of the Psalms when it comes to devotion and spirituality. I want to complement the more traditional, person-centered, psychologically-oriented approach with an explicitly theological approach, as described above.

Jesus in a new way. For other works that have connected the Psalms to justice-seeking and peacemaking, see Pleins, *Psalms*; Westermeyer, *Let Justice Sing*.

6. Calvin, *Commentary on the Book of Psalms*, xxxvii.

7. Luther, "Preface to the Psalter," 256.

8. Endres, "Psalms and Spirituality," 150. For an insightful account of how this approach to the Psalms has nurtured a vibrant spirituality, see also Davis, *Opening Israel's Scriptures*, 312–34.

A primary motivation for this desire is simple—that is, the persistent and pervasive presence of injustice, unrighteousness, and the lack of *shalom* in our world. For instance, in the United States of America, perhaps the richest nation in the history of the world, approximately one in six children is regularly hungry, malnourished, or food-insecure. This is outrageously unjust. As actor and hunger activist Jeff Bridges puts it:

> Thirty-five million people in the US are hungry or don't know where their next meal is coming from, and thirteen million of them are children. If another country were doing this to our children, we'd be at war.[9]

The global statistics on poverty and hunger are similar, if not worse, especially in parts of Africa, Asia, and Latin America. Close to a billion people live daily with life-threatening poverty, while the richest 1 percent of the world's population owns 45 percent of the world's wealth and resources. And the gap between the richest and the poorest is growing steadily, both in the United States and the world. The problem is not, as many people are inclined to think, that the poor are not willing to work. Rather, there is a long history of colonizing oppression; there are systemic realities involving wages, taxes, trade agreements, labor laws, and more that guarantee that the rich will continue to prosper and the impoverished will stay poor.

One of the systemic realities is the pervasiveness of racism in the United States and elsewhere. I live in St. Louis County, Missouri, and one of our county's suburbs, Ferguson, became virtually synonymous with systemic injustice after the murder of Michael Brown in 2014. As the US Department of Justice and the Ferguson Commission have made clear, people of color in Ferguson have been discriminated against, racially profiled, entrapped in a manifestly unfair and unjust legal system, and deprived of access to educational and economic opportunity as well as adequate health care. And as we are coming to realize, Ferguson is not unique. As

---

9. "Quotes about Hunger" (www.hungerhike.org).

Leah Gunning Francis puts it, "There is a Ferguson Near You."[10] Unfortunately, more recent events demonstrate the persistence of systemic racism and the truth of Gunning Francis's conclusion—Cleveland, Minneapolis, Louisville, Atlanta, Brunswick, Georgia. The list goes on, and we can "say their names"—Tamir Rice, George Floyd, Breonna Taylor, Rayshard Brooks, Ahmaud Arbery, and unfortunately all too many more.

And as if all this were not enough, the creation itself is under duress. The earth is warming at an unprecedented rate; species are disappearing with a frequency perhaps a thousand times greater than they have in the course of natural history; and we human beings are consuming at a rate that would take the resources of four or five earths to sustain in the long run. Our current practices of production, consumption, and relating to each other and the earth are unsustainable. The creation itself cries out for justice, righteousness, and *shalom*.

Obviously, these realities are profoundly challenging, even overwhelming. But it will do no good to ignore them. My point, to be demonstrated from the Psalms, is that God cares about these realities, because God claims the world and all its peoples as God's own. To put it pointedly, from the perspective of the Psalms (and the Bible as a whole), the realities named above are *spiritual* issues. Yes, they may be social, economic, scientific, ecological, and political issues, but they are manifestly *spiritual* issues as well, about which God cares and concerning which God is at work in the world.

The question is this: Where are we at work in the world? In the final analysis, of course, even though I am insisting that spirituality is fundamentally God-centered, we human beings are intimately involved. Indeed, the most spiritual thing we can do is to join God at God's work in the world, identifying where injustice and unrighteousness exist, and moving ourselves, the human community, and the creation toward the *shalom*, the peace or "comprehensive well-being," that God wills. And the most

---

10. Francis, *Ferguson and Faith*, 123. For more on Ferguson and its aftermath, see Francis, *Faith after Ferguson*.

spiritual thing we can do will need always to be accompanied by the most spiritual thing we can say, "I am for peace" (Ps 120:7).[11]

Discussion Questions

1. To set the tone for studying this volume, listen to Richard Bruxvoort Colligan's psalm-song for Psalm 120, "I Am for Peace" (available on iTunes and other music platforms), which was inspired in part by events in Ferguson, MO. How does the song help you think about injustices in the world? Where is the "Ferguson Near You"?

2. Where and how do you hear spirituality being talked about nowadays? Where and how does the Holy Spirit fit in to your understanding of spirituality?

3. Why haven't the Psalms typically been understood in connection with the pursuit of justice and peace?

---

11. For a compelling and powerful musical interpretation of Psalm 120, see (and listen to) Richard Bruxvoort Colligan, "I Am For Peace (Psalm 120)."

1

"The Single Most Important Text in the Entire Christian Bible"[1]

WHAT IS THE MOST important text in the Bible? The likely answers might include texts like John 1:14 ("And the Word became flesh and lived among us") or John 3:16, Psalm 23, or perhaps several non-numerical responses like the Golden Rule, the Beatitudes, or the Sermon on the Mount (which contains the Beatitudes and the Golden Rule). If we could manage to ask every Christian in the world this question, it is likely that not a single one would answer, "Psalm 82."

Actually, at least one person would. We know this because this person has, and he is a notable exception because he is one of the most well-known biblical scholars in the United States and the world. He is New Testament scholar John Dominic Crossan, and in his book *The Birth of Christianity: Discovering What Happened in the Years Immediately after the Execution of Jesus*, Crossan concludes that Psalm 82 "is the single most important text in the entire Christian

---

1. Crossan, *Birth of Christianity*, 575. The title of this chapter is a quote from Crossan.

Bible."[2] Even if one concludes that Crossan is exaggerating—or just plain wrong—we owe Psalm 82 a very careful look.

Psalm 82

Psalm 82 is unique in the book of Psalms. It fits none of the traditional categories that we shall examine in the subsequent chapters. Rather, it is a poetic narrative in which the God of Israel interrupts a meeting of the Canaanite gods and goddesses, then proceeds to put them on trial (v. 1). The charges against the Canaanite deities appear in vv. 2–4. They have not done justice (v. 2). The shape of the justice and righteousness that they should have done is spelled out very clearly in vv. 3–4. Justice and righteousness consist of careful attention to and provision for those whose lives are most threatened—"the weak and the orphan . . . the lowly and the destitute" (v. 3), "the weak and the needy" (v. 4). Instead of setting things right for the vulnerable, the gods and goddesses have acted as patrons of the rich and powerful, here called simply "the wicked" (vv. 2, 4).

The catastrophic effect of the injustice of the gods and goddesses is described in v. 5: "All the foundations of the earth are shaken." This description partakes of the ancient view of the cosmos, in which the mountains were "the foundations of the earth" that held up the sky (thus holding back the waters above) and that anchored the dry land in place (thus keeping in check the waters below). In this cosmological view, the worst-case scenario is that the mountains shake, releasing the waters above and below. The ordered cosmos reverts to a watery chaos! In short, the injustice of the gods and goddesses threatens the world with destruction.

In essence, v. 5 serves as the verdict in the trial. Because of their injustice that is destroying the world, the gods and goddesses are clearly guilty. The sentencing phase of the trial is found in vv. 6–7. The gods and goddesses are deposed; they are demoted to the status of human beings, thus they are subject to death "like

2. Crossan, *Birth of Christianity*, 575. See also McCann, "Single Most Important Text in the Bible," 63–75.

mortals" (v. 7). The final verse of Psalm 82 is a prayer to the God of Israel:

> Arise, O God, establish justice on earth,
> for all the nations are your possession. (my translation)

In short, the prayer is that the God of Israel do what the gods and goddesses have failed to do—justice! The justice of Israel's God will be world-encompassing because all nations belong to God. So, the whole world will be safe and secure.

Why is Psalm 82 so extraordinarily important? Crossan explains, as follows:

> [Psalm 82] is, for me, more important than John 1:14, which speaks of the Word of God becoming flesh and living among us. Before celebrating that incarnation, we must address a prior question about the character of the divinity involved. And that short psalm best summarizes for me the character of the Jewish God as Lord of all the world. . . . [The Canaanite deities] are dethroned for injustice, for divine malpractice, for transcendental malfeasance in office. They are rejected because they do not demand and effect justice among the peoples of the earth.
> . . . Psalm 82 tells us how we are to be judged by God *but also how God wants to be judged by us.* Everything that God says or does in Bible or life should be judged by that job description. Is this or that the transcendental justice defined in Psalm 82 at work? Or is this or that just transcendental testosterone?[3]

In other words, Psalm 82 offers the clearest biblical description of what it means to be divine; Psalm 82 defines "god-ness." The fundamental criterion for divinity is not simply power. Rather, it is justice, defined explicitly as provision for the life and health of the human community of all nations, especially provision for those least able to help themselves. To put it very plainly, biblically speaking, justice is not giving people what they deserve. Rather, it is giving everyone what they need.

3. Crossan, *Birth of Christianity*, 575–76 (emphasis added).

This is extraordinary! Let's return to the definition of spirituality that I offered in the introduction: "Spirituality is the work of God the Holy Spirit in our lives . . . calling us to the service of God's righteousness in the world." According to Psalm 82, the "work of God," to which God is calling us, is quintessentially justice. Spirituality and justice are inseparable; insofar as spirituality involves us human beings, and it does, it means that we will find ourselves called to do what God does in the world—justice!

As suggested in the introduction, the keyword in Psalm 82 is *justice*, although the standard translations obscure its four-fold repetition. The Hebrew root involved occurs in v. 1 ("judgment"); in v. 2 ("judge"); in v. 3 ("Give justice"); and finally in v. 8 ("judge," although my translation is "establish justice," as suggested above). The Hebrew poets regularly employ repetition to emphasize what is important; in this case, it is *justice*! And because the God of Israel is the God of "all the nations" (v. 8), the justice that God wills and works for is world-encompassing. This, too, is extraordinary! So often, people of faith are inclined to claim that "God is on our side." But such a claim will only be correct when those making it are servants of those whom God is intent upon protecting and providing for—"the weak and the orphan . . . the lowly and the destitute" (v. 3), and "the weak and the needy" (v. 4), of whatever nationality and wherever on earth they happen to be.[4]

Why Psalm 82 Is Not Simply Imperialistic: Psalm 89

In our pluralistic world, in which we are rightly sensitive to the importance of interfaith relationships, Psalm 82 may sound

4. For a thorough scholarly interpretation of Psalm 82, including translation issues, language, structure, ancient Near Eastern background and parallels, history of interpretation, and more, see Mongé-Greer, *Divine Council, Ethics, and Resistance.* Her basic conclusions are entirely congruent with my own. As she says, "The issue central to the psalm is one of justice for the poor and marginalized in society. . . . It is a message of advocacy and hope for those who pursue justice. . . . The appeal of implicit ethics in Psalm 82 is a calling to persons at every level to respond and take a stand for right justice" (194, 196).

dangerously imperialistic—that is, our God is better than your god(s), and our God will put your god(s) out of business! We should not dismiss this danger too easily, given the propensity that we named above—that is, the temptation to claim in an unqualified way that "God is on our side" (which, of course, always implies that God is not on your side, whoever the "your" happens to be). So, I want to acknowledge the possible danger and the need for caution; however, we should also be aware that the book of Psalms itself provides a way to prevent the mistake of imperialism. The preventative action is Psalm 89, which concludes Book III of the Psalter, in which Psalm 82 appears. The first thirty-seven verses of Psalm 89 describe at length the covenant relationship between God and the Davidic dynasty (see "covenant" in vv. 3, 28, 34) that is supposed to last "forever" (vv. 4, 28, 29, 36, 37). As we shall see in chapter 3, the Davidic kings were viewed as God's "son" (see Ps 2:7; 2 Sam 7:14), and their responsibility was to enact on earth the justice and righteousness that God wills for the world (see Psalm 72).

But what Psalm 89 suggests, beginning in v. 38, is that God has rejected the Davidic dynasty, presumably because of its failure to do justice and righteousness, as the prophets regularly had warned would be the case. Verse 39 puts it bluntly: "You have renounced the covenant with your servant." Again, this is extraordinary! In short, God will renounce and reject *God's own son* when that son fails to do the justice and righteousness with which he has been entrusted. Or, to put it slightly differently, God plays no favorites; God shows no partiality *except* to favor justice and righteousness. As we have seen, the commitment to and pursuit of justice and righteousness are what constitutes authentic divinity. Similarly, the commitment to and pursuit of justice and righteousness are what constitutes faithfulness among human beings. Again, the clear implication is that justice and spirituality—being called and empowered to join God at God's work in the world—are inseparable.

Psalm 82 Today

Whereas John Dominic Crossan leads us to see that Psalm 82 is among the most important texts in the Bible, if not *the* most important, John Goldingay suggests that Psalm 82 "stands as one of the most *worrying* texts in the OT."[5] He is certainly correct; and to appreciate why he is correct, we return to v. 5. To be sure, we contemporary readers do not view the cosmos in the same way that the ancient psalmist did. Even so, the psalmist's assessment of the effects of injustice is strikingly contemporary. Here is how the psalmist put it:

> They have neither knowledge nor understanding,
> > they walk around in darkness;
> > all the foundations of the earth are shaken.

Now, if we transpose the psalmist's claim for our time and place, it would go something like this: "In the presence of pervasive, systemic injustice, especially when injustice is given a religious sanction, chaos will reign." Or, as Eugene Peterson renders the final line of v. 5 in *The Message*:

> And now everything's falling apart,
> > the world's coming unglued.[6]

Although expressed in ancient cosmological terms, the psalmist's assessment sounds as timely as today's headlines. And, of course, this is precisely what is so worrisome!

We do not have to look far to see chaotic conditions that make us wonder whether things are falling apart or coming unglued:

- The unconscionable rates of poverty, hunger, malnutrition, food-insecurity, and homelessness in the United States and the world.

- The fact that 663 million people in the world do not have access to clean, safe water.

---

5. Goldingay, *Psalms*, 570 (emphasis added).
6. Peterson, *Message*, 663.

- The obscene and growing gap between the wealthy and the impoverished in the United States and the world.

- The long-standing, systemic racism that many people refuse to acknowledge, much less begin to address.

- The migration and immigration crisis: there are currently 70.8 million forcibly displaced persons in the world—41.3 million internally displaced persons, 25.9 million refugees, and 3.5 million asylum seekers, thousands of whom are regularly detained at the southern border of the United States and are treated in an utterly inhumane manner.

- Ongoing discrimination against LGBTQIA+ folk that is often hatefully and violently expressed.

- The fact that 40.5 million people in the world are victims of human trafficking, including 4.5 million in the United States, many of whom are children and are sexually exploited.

- Mass shootings that occur so regularly now that we are hardly surprised, although always shocked.

- Epidemic violence in the streets of virtually every urban area (and elsewhere).

- 12 million orphaned children on the continent of Africa (recall the mention of "the orphan" in Ps 82:3), due to rates of AIDS approaching 25 percent of the population in several African nations.

- Enduring hostility and violence in the Middle East.

- Irrefutable evidence that human activity is causing the earth's temperature to rise steadily, with potentially catastrophic results, some of which have already begun.

- Unprecedented rates of the disappearance of plant and animal species, due primarily to loss of habitat and climate change.

Unfortunately, the list could go on. We can only hope that Psalm 82, along with other psalms and biblical texts, will be worrisome enough to impel us to confront the troubling realities of our world. To be sure, an understandable response might be anxiety, fear, and hopelessness. But the response invited by Psalm 82, along with the rest of the Psalter and the Bible, is to identify injustice, to pray for justice (see Ps 82:8), and to join God at God's work in the world. Indeed, such is the essence of spirituality!

Discussion Questions

1. Almost no one would think of Psalm 82 as "the single most important text in the entire Christian Bible." What do you think? In your opinion, what are some other pivotally important texts, and how might they relate to Psalm 82?

2. Consider the importance of understanding that an essential element of God's character is not only power but also justice. Latin American and other liberation theologians affirm God's "preferential option for the poor." What do you think?

3. Why is it so important that the justice that God wills is world-encompassing? Listen and watch Richard Bruxvoort Colligan's psalm-song based on Psalm 82, "Real Justice" (available on YouTube). How does it help you appreciate the expansiveness of God's justice?

4. Consider Eugene Peterson's translation of Ps 82:5. In your opinion, how is the world "falling apart" or coming "unglued"? What can we do about it?

2

God "Has Come to Establish Justice"

The Enthronement Psalms

IF PSALM 82 WERE the only psalm in the Psalter that portrayed God's work in the world as justice and righteousness, then we might safely conclude that this rather unique psalm is an anomaly. But such is clearly *not* the case! To demonstrate this fact, we turn now to a group of psalms known as the enthronement psalms, because each of these psalms either refers to God as "King" (Hebrew *melek*; see 29:10; 47:2, 6, 7, 8; 95:3; 98:6; 99:4) or affirms that God "reigns" (my translation; NRSV "is king"), using a verbal form of the Hebrew root *mlk* (see 93:1; 96:10; 97:1; 99:1). The entire list of enthronement psalms includes Psalms 29, 47, 93, 95–99, but we shall focus on Psalms 96–99, which seem to be the concluding core of an enthronement collection consisting of Psalms 93, 95–99.

Before examining these psalms in more detail, it is to be noted that the enthronement collection occupies a particularly important place in the Psalter. As we saw in chapter 1, Book III of the Psalter ends with Psalm 89, which relates the rejection of the Davidic dynasty and the failure of the Davidic covenant. Historically speaking, the moment in view is the destruction of Jerusalem by the Babylonians in 587 BCE, marking the beginning of the Babylonian exile. This event was a monumental social, economic, political, and theological crisis. God's city, Jerusalem, was destroyed; the temple, God's house and a hub of both religious and economic activity, was leveled; and the Davidic king, God's "son," was deposed and taken into captivity. It appeared that everything was lost and there would be no future for God's people (see the people's laments in Isa 40:27; Ezek 37:11).

In light of Book III, which ends with the despairing cry of the deposed Davidic monarch (Ps 89:46–51), Book IV seems to be designed to offer a response to the crisis. Psalm 90, the first psalm in Book IV, is the only psalm in the entire Psalter that is attributed to Moses. This is important because Moses had interceded for the people at an earlier point in their story when it seemed like they were doomed (see Exod 32:1–14), and because Moses had presided over the people of God before they had any of the things that were lost in the year 587. Recall that Moses led the people before they possessed a land, before there was a temple, and before there was a monarchy. The message is clear enough—that is, relationship with God is still possible even without land, temple, or earthly king.

Continuing this direction, the enthronement collection is the most obvious structural feature of Book IV, and its repeated affirmation of God's kingship has a decidedly Mosaic ring to it (see Exod 15:18). The affirmation of God's kingship also begins to address the question of what the people will do, given the loss of the monarchy. In short, God will be their king, just as God was recognized as the sole king of the people in the pre-monarchic era (see Judg 8:23; 1 Sam 8:1–18).

Because of the pivotal placement and significance of the enthronement collection, Book IV has rightly been called the "editorial 'center'"[1] of the Psalter; and the enthronement collection has been called its "theological 'heart.'"[2] This means that Book IV and the enthronement collection deserve particularly careful attention; for our purposes, it is especially important that, like Psalm 82, the core of the enthronement collection (Psalms 96–99) describes God's work in the world as justice and righteousness. The nearly

---

1. Wilson, *Editing of the Hebrew Psalter*, 215.

2. Wilson, "Use of Royal Psalms," 92.

identical conclusions of Psalms 96 and 98 are particularly pertinent in this regard, so we shall begin with them.

Psalms 96 and 98

Before looking at the nearly identical conclusions of Psalms 96
and 98, it is to be noted that they also begin with identical opening lines: "O sing to the LORD a new song." What exactly is this
"new song"? We do not know for sure, but given the likelihood that
the enthronement collection is intended to respond to the crisis
of exile, the "new song" is probably meant to be understood as a
song of praise in response to the good news that God was bringing
the exile to an end. Historically speaking, the moment was 539
BCE, after the Persians had defeated the Babylonians, and after the
Persian king, Cyrus, had issued an edict that allowed the exiles to
return home to the land of Judah and the city of Jerusalem, and to
rebuild the temple (see Ezra 1:2–5; 2 Chr 36:22–23).

Scholars have long noted a similarity between Psalms 96–99
(especially Psalms 96 and 98) and Isaiah 40–55, the portion of
the book of Isaiah that derives from about 539 BCE and begins
with the good news that the exile is over (Isa 40:1–2), that the
people can return home (Isa 40:3–5), and that God continues
to be present among God's people (Isa 40:9; see "good tidings"
twice in 40:9, and note that "tell" in Ps 96:2 is more accurately
"proclaim good tidings"). In short, in the midst of the chaos of
defeat and exile, God is doing something new; and this new thing
invites the singing of a "new song." Not surprisingly, Isa 42:9 explicitly mentions the "new things" that God is doing, and the next
verse, Isa 42:10, is identical to Pss 96:1a and 98:1a: "Sing to the
LORD a new song."

The deliverance from captivity that God was effecting for
God's people—the "new things"—is what both Psalms 96 and 98
refer to with the same Hebrew word, translated "marvelous works"
in Ps 96:2 and "marvelous things" in Ps 98:1. This same Hebrew
word also appears in the song that Moses and the Israelites sang to
celebrate their deliverance from captivity in Egypt (see "wonders"

in Exod 15:11). This Hebrew root and its pattern of occurrences put an emphasis on God's activity, God's work (and recall again the definition of spirituality offered in the introduction: "Spirituality is the work of God the Holy Spirit . . ."); the focus on God's work invites us to pay particular attention to how the conclusions of both Psalms 96 and 98 describe what God is doing in the world.

As suggested above, Pss 96:13 and 98:9 are nearly identical. In the traditional translations, both of these verses proclaim that God "is coming to judge the earth." This translation is misleading in two ways. First, the phrase "is coming" almost inevitably is heard by readers as something that will happen in the future. And second, the translation "judge" almost inevitably communicates something negative, as if God is angry and out to get even. But there are much better translations of this proclamation. The verb that the traditional translations render as "is coming" does *not* indicate a future event. Grammatically speaking, the verb form is either a present active participle, which can indicate current and ongoing action, or it is what is known in Hebrew as a perfect form, which ordinarily indicates a completed action (and thus is usually rendered in English as a past tense). As for the phrase, "to judge the earth," it can also be accurately rendered, "to establish justice on earth" (my translation; see the CEB).

Putting all this together, we arrive at two possible renderings of the proclamation in Pss 96:13 and 98:9, as follows: (1) God "is (currently in the process of) coming to establish justice on earth," or (2) God "has come to establish justice on earth." Either one of these is better than the traditional translations, but given the celebrative tone of both psalms, including the opening invitation to "sing to the LORD a new song" and several subsequent invitations to praise, it is likely that the second option above is to be preferred. In short, a new song is to be sung; God is to be praised because God "has come to establish justice on earth."

To expand a bit, I offer the following translations of Pss 96:12b–13 and 98:9:

Surely all the trees of the forest sing for joy
   before the LORD; for he has come;
   for he has come to establish justice on earth.
He establishes justice in the world with righteousness,
   and among the peoples with his faithfulness.
   (Ps 96:12b–13; my translation)

The floods clap their hands;
   the hills sing joyfully together before the LORD,
   for he has come to establish justice on earth.
He establishes justice in the world with righteousness,
   and among the peoples with equity.
   (Ps 98:9; my translation)

There are several crucial things to notice, all of which reinforce the portrayal of God, God's will, and God's work that we saw in Psalm 82. First, recall that Psalm 82 considers the commitment to and the establishment of justice to be an essential aspect of divinity or "god-ness." It concluded with a prayer for God to "establish justice on earth," and this is exactly what Psalms 96 and 98 proclaim that God has come to do. The repetition of "establish justice" in Pss 96:13 and 98:9 adds further emphasis. And just as Ps 82:3 pairs justice and righteousness ("Give justice . . . maintain the right"), so do Pss 96:13 and 98:9. As suggested above, justice and righteousness are virtually synonymous and frequently paired together. We shall see this pairing again in Psalm 72 in the next chapter.

Second, as we saw in the previous chapter, Psalm 82 is expansive in its perspective. The God of Israel was deeply concerned because the gods and goddesses were destroying "the earth" (Ps 82:5). The prayer that concludes Psalm 82 is a prayer for justice for "the earth," including "all the nations." Psalms 96 and 98 are similarly expansive. In Psalm 96, the "families of the peoples" are invited to worship God (v. 7), as is "all the earth" (v. 9). Psalm 98 also invites "all the earth" to praise God (v. 4). And in both psalms, the celebration of God's having come to establish justice includes the whole creation (96:11–13; 98:7–9). In short, what we are to conclude is that God wills and works for justice and righteousness on nothing short of a creation-encompassing scale.

Third, in an affirmation that is again expansive and that explicitly recalls Psalm 82, Ps 96:10 proclaims: "The world is firmly established; it shall never be moved." In contrast to the gods and goddesses whose injustice destabilized and threatened the earth with destruction (Ps 82:5; "shaken" in Ps 82:5 and "moved" in Ps 96:10 are the same Hebrew root), God's having come to establish justice puts the world on a stable foundation, thus offering a secure future. This affirmation is, therefore, a further indication of the quintessential significance of justice, in terms of understanding God, God's will, and God's work. Even further indication is found in Psalms 97 and 99, the other two psalms that are part of the core of the enthronement collection.

Psalms 97 and 99

With these two psalms, we can be much briefer. The similar opening lines and conclusions of Psalms 96 and 98 give them particular prominence in the enthronement collection, but we should note at least briefly that Psalms 97 and 99 join Psalms 96 and 98 in associating justice and righteousness with God's character, will, and work. In Psalm 97, this is explicit in the affirmation of v. 2b that "righteousness and justice are the foundation of his throne." Righteousness is mentioned again in v. 6, "The heavens proclaim his righteousness," and "judgments" in v. 8 could better be translated "acts of justice" (my translation). As for Psalm 99, God is a "lover of justice," and has "executed justice and righteousness in Jacob" (v. 4). The cumulative effect is clear. In continuity with Psalm 82, the enthronement collection affirms that God's work consists quintessentially of establishing justice and setting things right on a world-encompassing scale.

The Enthronement Psalms Today

It is perhaps easy to see how the message of Psalms 96–99 would have been good news in their ancient context—that is, to exiled Judeans whose lives had been chaotically disrupted, it would have been good news to hear that God was still sovereign, that God had come to establish justice on earth and to set things right. But what about us, and what about today? As suggested at the end of chapter 1, our world seems to resemble more closely the description of Ps 82:5 than that of Ps 96:10—that is, things look more like they are perilously close to "falling apart" and "coming unglued" rather than "firmly established" and permanently stable. So, what do we make of the affirmation that God reigns, that God has come to establish justice and righteousness on earth, when it does not appear that this is the case?

We could conclude, of course, that the psalmists were just wrong. For Christians, however, this is a particularly problematic conclusion, since the fundamental message of the enthronement psalms is essentially the same as Jesus' basic message: "The time is fulfilled, and the kingdom of God has come near; repent, and believe in the good news" (Mark 1:15). In short, God reigns!

Rather than conclude that the psalmists were wrong, however, there is another option—and Jesus' invitation to repent is a crucial clue. It is crucial because it suggests that God does not exercise God's sovereignty as sheer force. Rather, God invites our commitment and response. God is present, and God's will for the world—justice, righteousness, and peace—is clear. But if we do not cooperate, God's will does not get done! In other words, God has chosen not to operate unilaterally; rather, God has chosen to work incarnationally. God's power is not sheer force. It is sheer love!

We might wish that God would simply make things right, but such coercion would violate the essential relatedness between God and humankind. As Douglas John Hall suggests, love that is programmed would not be love. For love's sake, for the sake of genuine relatedness with humankind, God gives us freedom and invites our faithful response. The implementation of God's work in the world depends on our response. As Hall puts it, this is God's "Great Risk," because it means that we can thwart God's will.[3] And, of course, we often have—and we often do.

The realities that we mentioned at the end of chapter 1—poverty, hunger, and homelessness; racism and various forms of hateful discrimination; hostility and violence; ecological distress; and more—are not God's will. Neither are they the result of God's failure to be present or failure to act. God is present, and God has shown us how to act justly, rightly, peacefully, and faithfully. But when we fail to enact and embody God's will for the world, the results are and always will be chaotic and destructive. Current realities show us that we are perfectly capable of ignoring God's will, hurting ourselves and others, and endangering the earth and its future.

This, of course, makes it all the more important that we think about spirituality fundamentally as *God's* work, including God's work of preparing us to be servants of God's justice, righteousness, and peace. In the next chapter, we shall see how in Old Testament times, the Judean kings were called to be the earthly agents of God's justice, righteousness, and peace. When they failed, God extended the call to the whole people of God. God is still calling the whole people of God to be servants of God's work in the world. Indeed, such is the essence of spirituality!

Discussion Questions

1. What are the possible advantages and disadvantages of the image of God as "king"?

2. How do you think about and describe the power of God?

3. What difference does it make to say that God "has come" into the world?

4. Isaac Watts's metrical version of Psalm 98 is the familiar and beloved hymn, "Joy to the World." Why and how is it

3. Douglas John Hall, *God and Human Suffering*, 70.

meaningful and appropriate to sing Psalm 98 at Christmas? Does singing Psalm 98 at Christmas help you appreciate the conclusion that God works incarnationally, and what difference does this make? How can the celebration of Christmas be an occasion for justice-seeking and peacemaking?

3

Agents of God's Justice

The Royal Psalms

As we have seen, Psalm 82 defines "god-ness" in a way that makes the unwavering commitment to and enactment of justice and righteousness—understood as attention to and provision for those whose lives are most threatened and vulnerable—an essential component of it. And the enthronement psalms, especially Psalms 96 and 98, affirm that God "has come . . . to establish justice in the world with righteousness" (Pss 96:13; 98:9; my translation). The question, which was raised indirectly at the end of chapter 2, is this: How will this happen in real time among real people in real places?

The Old Testament, including—or perhaps especially—the book of Psalms, proposes an answer to this question. It was the responsibility of the earthly king to enact the royal policy of the heavenly king—justice, righteousness, and peace. Before we turn to Psalm 72, the key text in this regard, we need to notice that the book of Psalms affords a great deal of attention to the earthly monarch. Not only do seventy-three psalms contain in their titles the name *David*, the most famous king and progenitor of the dynasty that ruled the united kingdoms and the southern kingdom of Judah for over four hundred years, but also royal psalms appear at strategic places in the Psalter. For instance, Psalm 2 joins Psalm 1 as a paired introduction to the book of Psalms. Notice that neither Psalm 1 nor Psalm 2 contains a title, and the two are bound by the repetition of "Happy" in 1:1 and 2:12. Their relationship is further indicated by other words that occur in both psalms ("meditate" in 1:2 and "plot" in 2:1, which represent the same Hebrew root; "way" in 1:6 twice and again in 2:12; and "perish" in 1:6 and 2:12).

So, right from the outset, we learn that the earthly king is very important. He is God's "anointed" (the Hebrew word is usually transliterated as *messiah*), and in 2:6, the divine voice announces that the "anointed" is "my king." The special relationship between God, the heavenly king, and God's "anointed," the earthly king, is made even clearer in 2:7, when the earthly king relates that God has "said to me, 'You are my son; today I have begotten you.'" The conversation between God and God's son has the character of a liturgical exchange, and the "today" of v. 7 may have been the day a new king was crowned or perhaps the day that marked the anniversary of a king's reign. In any case, we learn from Psalm 2 that the king was viewed as nothing less than God's son (see also 2 Sam 7:14).

As God's earthly representative or agent, the king had a certain job to do. Although the language of Ps 2:8-9 is violent, it suggests fundamentally that the king's job was to ensure that the nations of the earth conform to God's will (and as vv. 1-3 suggest, they were not inclined to do so!). The language of v. 11 is less violent, and the point is more obvious. The earthly king is to see to it that all other earthly kings and rulers "serve the LORD." Despite the violent language of vv. 8-9, the ultimate vision here is of a world united around the service of God's will, which, as the Psalter will later reveal (as we have seen), consists fundamentally of justice, righteousness, and peace.

The key placement of Psalm 2 anticipates the strategic placement of two more royal psalms—Psalm 72 at the conclusion of Book II (Psalms 42-72) and Psalm 89 at the end of Book III (Psalms 73-89). We have already examined Psalm 89 briefly. We now turn to Psalm 72, where the king's job as God's earthly agent is eminently clear. Not surprisingly, in light of Psalm 82, it centers on justice and righteousness, which result in *shalom*, "peace" or "comprehensive well-being" (my translation).

Psalm 72: The King's Job Description

Just as Psalm 2 probably originated as part of a coronation liturgy, so, too, did Psalm 72. Whereas Psalm 2 may have accompanied the act of crowning the king, Psalm 72 probably functioned as the coronation prayer as well as something like a charge to the new king. In any case, it is crucial to note the substance of what is prayed for—justice and righteousness. These two words are dominant in vv. 1–7, beginning in the first verse:

> Give the king your justice, O God,
>   and your righteousness to a king's son.

The Hebrew root underlying "justice" occurs again in v. 2 ("justice") and v. 4 ("defend the cause"), and a close synonym appears in v. 2 ("May he judge," or as it could be translated, "May he establish justice"). As we have seen in Psalms 82 and 96–99, as is often the case, "justice" and "righteousness" are paired in vv. 1 and 2. "Righteousness" occurs again in v. 3 and v. 7 (although the Hebrew form is more accurately "righteous one" in v. 7). The sheer repetition—three times for "justice" and four times for "righteousness"—effectively emphasizes the point. The earthly king's responsibility was to do what God wants done (Psalm 82); indeed, the king is to do what God "has come" to do (Psalms 96 and 98). This is a fundamentally incarnational responsibility. The king embodies or "fleshes out" the divine will on earth.

As in Psalm 82, doing justice and righteousness has everything to do with how the most vulnerable are treated. Already in vv. 1–4, the "poor" (vv. 2, 4) and "needy" (v. 4) receive particular attention. The king's responsibility toward them is even more clear in vv. 12–14. Indeed, vv. 12–14 suggest that the primary responsibility of the king is to protect and provide for the "needy" (v. 12 and twice in v. 13) and the "poor" (v. 12) along with "those who have no helper" (v. 12) and the "weak" (v. 13). There will be no justice nor will things be right unless the lives of the most vulnerable are valued and protected.

Justice + Righteousness = *Shalom* = Food

In addition to the words "justice" and "righteousness," the other keyword in Ps 72:1–7 is *shalom*. We did not encounter the word *shalom* in Psalms 82, 96–99, but *shalom* belongs with and occurs elsewhere in passages that feature "justice" and "righteousness" (see, for instance, Isa 32:16–17). In fact, it is accurate to say that *shalom* describes the reality of a situation in which justice and righteousness are enacted and embodied. The first occurrence of *shalom* in Psalm 72 is in v. 3, although the NRSV does not translate *shalom* as "peace" (as it usually does) but rather as "prosperity," as follows:

> May the mountains yield prosperity [*shalom*] for the people,
>   and the hills, in righteousness.

How do the mountains yield "peace" or "comprehensive well-being"? The mountains and hills are where the Judean people lived and thus where they had to grow their food. The clear implication is that *shalom* begins with having sufficient food to eat. Of course, this conclusion makes profoundly good sense for people who are poor and needy. Provision for the poor and needy begins with feeding them. And this, quintessentially, is the king's job!

Congruent with this interpretive direction is the imagery of vv. 5–7, especially v. 6, where the wish for the king is that "he be like rain that falls on the mown grass, like showers that water the earth." Why rain and showers? Because precipitation, especially in the relatively arid climate of the Judean hill country, is what makes the crops grow, meaning that food will be available. The population of Judah consisted overwhelmingly of peasant farmers, who strove mightily for simple subsistence. Food was of the essence. Not surprisingly, the second occurrence of *shalom* is in v. 7, which wishes that "peace abound" during the king's reign—that is, that sufficient food be available for everyone, because the king's administration has served like much-needed rain.

The agrarian dimension of Psalm 72 is evident as well in v. 16, where the psalmist's wish again involves abundant food: "May there be abundance of grain in the land; may it wave on the tops of the mountains." As in v. 3, "the mountains" are crucial as the location where food was grown. And, of course, food is crucial in providing for the people for whom the king is responsible, especially the poor, needy, and weak. *Shalom*, "peace" or "comprehensive well-being," begins with food. There will be no justice and things will not be right until everybody eats. God wills it, and it is the king's responsibility to see that it happens.

Because vv. 18–19 appear to be part of the concluding doxology for Book II (compare Pss 41:13; 89:52; 106:48), v. 17 marks the real conclusion of Psalm 72. The expansiveness of v. 17 is worth noting. The mention of "all nations" connects the conclusion of Psalm 72 to the conclusion of Psalm 82, and the expansiveness anticipates Pss 96:7–9 and 98:4–6, where the invitations to praise are world-encompassing. In view of the preceding content of Psalm 72, the implication is that God wills not only that the king provide for his own people but also that he feed the world. Verse 17b echoes Gen 12:1–3, where Abram is not only promised a blessing but also commissioned to effect a blessing for nothing short of "all the families of the earth." God's will for justice, righteousness, and peace knows no limits. God wills world-encompassing *shalom*, and this "comprehensive well-being" begins with food.[1]

A Note on Psalm 85: A *Shalom*-Description

The biblical connection between *shalom* and food is especially evident in Psalm 85. The psalm begins with the affirmation that God has "restored the fortunes of Judah" (v. 2); but according to vv. 4–7, the people stand in need again, and so they pray, "Restore us again" (v. 4). We do not know the situation that evoked this request, and we

---

1. For helpful discussions of 72:16 and 17, see Davis, *Scripture, Culture, and Agriculture*, 11, 165.

are not told whether the prayer was answered, but the psalmist certainly has hope that God "will speak peace to his people" (v. 8). The psalm concludes with a poetic description of the desired restoration. Verses 10–13 might be called a *shalom*-description.

In lovely poetic imagery, several key attributes of God's character and purposes are personified in vv. 10–11, 13—steadfast love (v. 10), faithfulness (vv. 10–11), righteousness (vv. 10, 13), and *shalom* (v. 10). The agricultural language of v. 11—"spring up from the ground"—anticipates a much more prosaic affirmation in v. 12:

> The LORD will give what is good,
> and our land will yield its increase.

The inclusion of this straightforward description of agricultural productivity, embedded as it is in the poetic portrayal of God's character and purposes, reinforces the message we detected in Psalm 72. In short, God's loving and faithful will for the world comes to very tangible expression when the land provides enough food for everyone to eat. This situation is "good," and it constitutes what is right. Again, the *shalom* that God wills begins with food; more specifically (especially in light of Psalm 72), it begins with sufficient food that is equitably distributed, so even the most vulnerable are provided for and will be able to eat.

The Demise of the Monarchy and the Rise of the People

Did the kings do what they were supposed to do? Did they protect the vulnerable? Did they provide food for the poor, the weak, and the needy? In a word, *no*; or, at least, they very seldom did so. Instead, the kings did what powerful people have done throughout history (and are still doing); that is, they used their power and resources to enrich themselves at the expense of others. The socio-economic mechanism was the appropriation of land from small farmers. This meant that peasant farmers lost the land they had used to grow food, while the king and the king's men had more land on which to grow cash crops for commercial purposes. The story of Naboth's Vineyard illustrates this dynamic all too clearly (see 1 Kgs 21:1–16).

The prophetic response (via the prophet Elijah) to the exploitation and death of Naboth at the hands of King Ahab indicates divine displeasure (1 Kgs 21:17–19), and several prophetic texts indicate that oppression of the weak by the powerful was widespread (see, for instance, Isa 1:10–20; 3:13–15; 5:1–10; 58:6–7; Amos 2:6–7; 3:9–11; 5:6–15; 6:1–7; Mic 2:1–5; 6:9–16).

It was precisely the failure of the monarchs to enact and embody God's will that called forth the prophets and their repeated attempts to call the kings and the royal bureaucracy to account. Ultimately, the prophets warned that the failure to do justice, righteousness, and peace would result in catastrophe. As suggested above, this is exactly what happened in 587 BCE with the destruction of Jerusalem and the disappearance of the monarchy (the northern kingdom, Israel, had been destroyed by the Assyrians in 721 BCE). The destruction is recounted in 2 Kings 25, but as suggested above (see chapter 1), the book of Psalms itself also reflects the demise of the monarchy, when, at a strategic point, Psalm 89 recounts the rejection of God's "anointed" and articulates the poignant cries and questions of an apparently deposed Davidic king (Ps 89:38–51).

Thus, Book III of the Psalter ends on a tragic note, to which the rest of the Psalter provides a response. Part of the immediate response in Book IV, as we saw above, is the message that God is still sovereign and is in the process of doing new things. Even so, a critical question was this: Given the loss of the monarchy, who or what will be the earthly agent to enact and embody God's will for justice, righteousness, and *shalom*?

To be sure, after the exile and the return to Judah and Jerusalem, some people expected the restoration to include, at least eventually, a restored monarchy. It is even possible that the Psalter preserves such expectations since it includes royal psalms in Books IV and V (see Psalms 101, 110, 132, 144); but the hope for a restored Davidic monarchy seems to have been dampened in the final form of the Psalter. For instance, while Psalm 132 recalls the promises to David and his descendants (vv. 11–12), it indicates that David seems to be having a difficult time, so much so that his enemies seem to have the upper hand (vv. 17–18). The same is true of Psalm 144, which recalls the earlier Psalm 18, in which David was clearly victorious over his foes. But in Psalm 144, David stands in need of rescue "from the hand of aliens" (v. 11). Given the ongoing adversity of "David" in the postexilic era and the historical fact that the Davidic monarchy never reappeared, it is likely that the people of God arrived at a different answer to the question of earthly agency.

Who is responsible for enacting and embodying the will of God in the world? *We* are! There is evidence for this move in the book of Isaiah, chapters 40–55, the portion of the book that derives from the early postexilic era and may reflect attitudes of an even later time. In Isa 55:3–5, the "everlasting covenant" that God is making is with *the whole people*, not with David. The people as a whole will fulfill the function formerly assigned to the Davidic monarchy. As Edgar Conrad puts it, the book of Isaiah envisions a "world of democratized kingship in which the people are addressed as kings."[2]

The book of Psalms reinforces this direction as it moves toward its conclusion. Psalm 149 clearly recalls Psalm 2, but the job of implementing God's will among the nations (compare Ps 2:8–9 with Ps 149:6–9) belongs not to the king; rather, it belongs to God's "faithful ones" (v. 9; see "the faithful" in vv. 1, 5). It is even explicitly described in Psalm 149 as "justice" (v. 9; NRSV "judgment"). There is a king mentioned in Psalm 149, but it is clearly God (v. 2). The portrayal of God as king and the mention of "a new song" (v. 1) recall Psalms 96 and 98, effectively emphasizing God's kingship. This emphasis, along with the historical reality that a monarch never reappeared, serves to highlight the people's role. It became the responsibility of the whole people of God to enact and embody the justice, righteousness, and peace that God wills on earth.

To return to the book of Isaiah for a moment, it is likely that the servant mentioned or alluded to repeatedly in Isaiah 40–55, especially in the four Servant Songs (Isa 42:1–9; 49:1–6; 50:4–9;

2. Conrad, *Reading Isaiah*, 161.

52:13—53:12), is to be identified as the restored people of God. This suggests that an aspect of the "new things" God was doing (see Isa 42:9) was not only returning the people to Judah and Jerusalem but also giving them the new responsibility of fulfilling the function of the former monarchy. In this regard, it is to be noted that in the first Servant Song, the divine voice announces: "I have put my spirit upon him; he will bring forth justice to the nations" (42:1). In short, the people of God are empowered by the spirit to do God's work, and that work is justice on a world-encompassing scale, as it was in Psalm 72. The word "justice" is mentioned again in vv. 3 and 4; and again, the beneficiary of the establishment of justice is "the earth" (v. 4; see also v. 6, where the servant is to be "a light to the nations," as in Isa 49:6 as well). In short, the book of Isaiah and the book of Psalms converge at this point, suggesting that spirituality is (to return to our initial definition) the work of God among God's people, calling them to and preparing them for the "service of God's righteousness in the world."

The Royal Psalms Today

We have learned from the Psalms so far that "god-ness" is defined as commitment to and enactment of justice and righteousness for everyone in the world, measured by the comprehensive well-being (*shalom*) of the most vulnerable (Psalm 82). Such justice, righteousness, and peace are what God has come to do (Psalms 96 and 98). In this chapter, we have seen how God chose to accomplish God's will, working incarnationally through the earthly king and through the whole people of God. And God still works incarnationally, calling people to the service of God's work in the world. Indeed, such is the essence of spirituality.

Some Christians might suggest, however, that Jesus of Nazareth was the incarnation of God in the world (John 1:14), pointing out further that the expectations of a restored monarchy were fulfilled in Jesus, who bears the royal titles of "anointed" (Hebrew *messiah*; Greek *christos*) and "son of God." This is certainly true, in the sense that Jesus exercised royal power in a ministry of love and compassion focused on the needs of the least and lowly, including, of course, a ministry of feeding people. In other words, Jesus enacted and embodied kingship the way God intended it to be, so Christians affirm that Jesus is not just another *messiah* or son of God. Rather, he is *the Messiah* and *the* Son of God (see chapter 10).

Even so, Jesus himself did not do all the work in the world that needed to be done and needs to be done. He announced God's reign (as in Psalms 96–99), and he faithfully proclaimed and embodied God's character and will (as in Psalms 72 and 82). Jesus showed the way, and he invited people to follow. As the risen Christ, Jesus commissioned his followers to carry on God's work. The account in the Gospel of John is particularly revealing and pertinent for our purposes. Jesus says to his disciples, "Peace be with you" (John 20:19, 21), and he sends them out, equipped only by the Spirit: "He breathed on them and said to them, 'Receive the Holy Spirit'" (John 20:22). As Robin Scroggs suggests, what this remarkable scene means is that the church, empowered by the Spirit, becomes the ongoing "enfleshed logos" in the world, now that Jesus is no longer present in the flesh.[3] Christians properly affirm that Jesus is present, but he is present by way of the Spirit. The actual embodiment—the fleshing out—of God's character and will in the world involves us (or, in Pauline terms, we are "the body of Christ"; see 1 Cor 12:27). To be sure, God is at work in the world, but God is working incarnationally, by way of human agency. Our participation in God's work is what spirituality is all about.

To put it another way—since we have suggested that God's peace begins with food equitably distributed—there is still hunger in the world despite the fact that there is sufficient food for the current human population. The persistence of hunger is not the result of God's lack of concern or failure to act. It is the result of our failure, largely in the forms of greed and over-consumption. We know better. The Torah (Genesis-Deuteronomy) reveals a more faithful way; the Prophets call for a more faithful way; the Psalms present a more faithful way; and Jesus embodied and invited his followers to a more faithful way. The earth is capable

---

3. See Scroggs, *Christology in Paul and John*, 85–91 (esp. 85, 87–88, 90).

of producing sufficient food (at least for now, even when we do not care for it properly). God has done God's part. Will we do our part so that all people will be able to eat? To answer *Yes* to this question is at the heart of spirituality—discerning God's work in the world and responding to God's call to "the service of God's righteousness in the world."

Discussion Questions

1. Although the United States and many other parts of the world are no longer agrarian societies, food is still a basic necessity for everyone. How and why is it important that *shalom* begins with food?

2. James L. Mays has suggested that Psalm 72 is as close as the Bible comes to something like a blueprint for government. What would politics in the US and the world look like if Psalm 72 were a guide?

3. What does it mean to you that we as Christians are the ongoing "enfleshed logos" in the world?

4. How are you already at work feeding the hungry? If not doing so, how can you/we join God at God's work of feeding the world?

5. Listen to Richard Bruxvoort Colligan's psalm-song based on Psalm 72, "Be a Blessing" (available on YouTube, iTunes, and various music platforms). How does it help us realize that the responsibility of the ancient Israelite and Judean kings has become our calling as well?

4

The Pursuit of Happiness (and Justice!)

The Torah Psalms

BECAUSE PSALM 1 OBVIOUSLY comes first, and because scholars unanimously agree that Psalm 1 was either written or chosen to serve as the introduction to the book of Psalms, it would have made sense to begin this book with an interpretation of Psalm 1. I chose, however—primarily for emphasis and effect—to begin with "the single most important text in the entire Christian Bible." In the first three chapters, we have seen how Psalm 82, the enthronement psalms (especially Psalms 96 and 98), and the royal psalms (especially Psalm 72) portray justice, righteousness, and peace as the will of God for the world.

As we now approach Psalm 1, we are in a prime position to notice how Psalm 1 introduces the Psalter by inviting readers to look for clues concerning the will of God throughout the entire book. True, no translation of Psalm 1 includes the phrase "will of God." Rather, the operative word is *torah*, which occurs twice in v. 2 and which has traditionally been translated as "law." But the CEB has a much better translation of *torah*, as seen in its rendering of vv. 1–2:

> The truly happy person
>> doesn't follow wicked advice,
>> doesn't stand on the road of sinners,
>> and doesn't sit with the disrespectful.
> Instead of doing these things,
>> these persons love the LORD's Instruction,
>> and they recite God's Instruction day and night!

The Hebrew word *torah* does not mean "law." It means "teaching" or, as the CEB suggests, "instruction." Historically, God's people have discerned God's teaching in a written body of material—that is, Scripture, which does contain commandments that might properly be called "law." But Scripture also includes stories, declarations, affirmations, poems, genealogies, and more, all of which are capable of communicating something about God's character and purposes. This is one reason that "law" is much too narrow a rendering of *torah*. Then too, Scripture has not been the only source for discerning God's teaching. In fact, Jon Levenson suggests that for the Jewish tradition, *torah* can properly be understood to indicate something as broad as "unmediated divine teaching"[1] (a source of divine revelation that the United Church of Christ has highlighted prominently in recent years with its slogan, "God is Still Speaking").

From this perspective, *torah* is properly understood to be something like "the will of God." It is to be constantly discerned, not only in conversation with Scripture but also in conversation with the extensive body of Jewish and Christian tradition about how Scripture is to be interpreted as well as ongoing reflection about how our contemporary experience intersects with Scripture and tradition. In any case, the highlighting of *torah* at the very beginning of the Psalter alerts the reader to be attentive to how the Psalms themselves will serve as a source of instruction about God and God's will.

And we have already seen how this is clearly the case. Psalm 82 considers commitment to and enactment of justice

---

1. Levenson, "Sources of Torah," 570.

and righteousness to be *essential* to divinity; the enthronement psalms assert that God "has come to establish justice with righteousness"; and the royal psalms, along with Psalm 149, make it clear that the responsibility to do justice and righteousness in the world was entrusted to the earthly king and eventually to the whole people of God. By foregrounding *torah*—that is, God's will—Psalm 1 prepares the reader to attend carefully to the centrality of justice, righteousness, and peace; it also provides an incentive for doing so. In short, true happiness derives from a life fundamentally and constantly oriented to God's will. Or, in other words, true happiness derives from commitment to and enactment of justice, righteousness, and peace, defined (as God defines it) as attention to and provision for those whose lives are most threatened and most vulnerable. Or again, true happiness derives from joining God at God's work in the world, which is essentially how we have defined spirituality.

Given the introductory function of Psalm 1, it is not surprising that it specifically mentions "justice," although most translations use the English word "judgment," translating Ps 1:5 as follows:

Therefore the wicked will not stand in the judgment,
     nor sinners in the congregation of the righteous.

While this may be correct, it is problematic because it is not clear which judgment is being referred to here. Another possible rendering is this (my translation):

Therefore the wicked will not stand up for justice,
     nor sinners stand in the congregation of the righteous.

Why won't the wicked stand up for justice? Because unlike the happy/righteous person, they do not attend to God's instruction! And they will not "stand in the congregation of the righteous," not because they are being punished or excluded; rather, they simply refuse to come in. Their choice is ruinous, as v. 6 makes clear (just as the injustice of the gods and goddesses was ruinous in Psalm 82). They "perish," not because God is punishing them but simply because they have chosen injustice. As we have suggested, the results of injustice are, and always will be, chaotic and destructive (see above on Psalm 82, especially v. 5).

Whereas the wicked have no stable foundation—being blown about by the wind, according to v. 4—the happy/righteous person is portrayed as a solidly-rooted tree located by a source of water, thus able to live fruitfully and to "prosper" (v. 3). Actually, "prosper" is not a good translation; to contemporary North Americans, the word "prosper" almost inevitably connotes money or some form of material wealth. This is *not* the promise. As we shall see in the next chapter, the righteous are pervasively opposed and afflicted. A better translation perhaps would be "thrives" (see the JPS). In any case, the prosperity involved here consists essentially of connectedness to God, the ultimate source of life. Prosperity and happiness derive from entrusting life and future to God and, consequently, attending to God's will and joining God at God's work in the world, despite difficulty and opposition. Happiness will be experienced in the midst of the adversity, as the concluding line of Psalm 2 affirms: "Happy are all who take refuge in" God (Ps 2:12).

Happiness throughout the Psalter

The importance of the word "happy" is indicated not only by the fact that it is literally the first word in the Psalter, providing an envelope-structure for the first two psalms (1:1; 2:12), but also by the fact that it occurs twenty-four more times, including at several strategic places. For instance, "happy" occurs in every one of the final psalms in Books I–IV of the Psalter—Psalms 41, 72, 89, and 106. Psalm 41 begins with the line, "Happy are those who consider the poor." As we have seen, attentiveness to and provision for the poor and needy is precisely what God wills. And as we have also seen, attentiveness to the poor and needy is especially evident in Psalm 72, which concludes Book II. The king's primary responsibility was to consider the poor! And insofar as he did his job—which is described as justice, righteousness, and peace—the king would be a blessing to "all nations," who would in turn "pronounce him happy" (Ps 72:17). In Psalm 89, happiness is also associated with acknowledging and doing God's will. Verses 14–16 are as follows:

> Righteousness and justice are the foundations of your throne;
>   steadfast love and faithfulness go before you.
> Happy are the people who know the festal shout,
>   who walk, O LORD, in the light of your countenance;
> they exult in your name all day long,
>   and extol your righteousness.

In keeping with Psalms 96, 98, and the other enthronement psalms, God's reign is founded on justice and righteousness, according to Ps 89:14. The "festal shout" could have been a liturgical response; if so, it has profound behavioral implications. The Hebrew word behind "festal shout" occurs elsewhere in the context of affirmations of God's reign, and to acknowledge God's reign is to submit to God's will. The behavioral dimension is reinforced by the verb "walk" in v. 15. The Hebrew root is *hlk*, and the whole Jewish ethical tradition is known as the *halakah*, "The Walk" (compare the English saying, "Walking the walk, not just talking the talk"). The effect of Ps 89:14–16 is to say this: "Happy are those who do what amounts to the essence of God's will—justice and righteousness."

The occurrence of "happy" in Ps 106:3 is the most direct affirmation that happiness derives from doing God's will:

> Happy are those who observe justice,
>   who do righteousness at all times.

To be sure, most of the remainder of Psalm 106 is a very frank acknowledgment that the people of God have not done God's will (see especially vv. 6–46), but what they should have done as a matter of their covenant relationship with God (see Psalm 105) is clear from the beginning. They should have done justice and righteousness, which would have yielded true happiness, as opposed to their actual behavior that had evoked God's angry response (see v. 40).

It is true that the concluding psalm of Book V, Psalm 150, does not include the word "happy." But it may not be coincidental that Psalm 146, which initiates a collection of hallelujah psalms (Psalms 146–50, all of which begin and end with *hallelu-yah*, "Praise the LORD"), does mention "happy" (v. 5) for a final time in the Psalter:

> Happy are those whose help is in the God of Jacob,
>   whose hope is in the LORD their God.

Psalm 146 continues with a rehearsal of what God has done and does. The list includes the affirmation that God "executes justice for the oppressed" (v. 7), "watches over the strangers," and "upholds the orphan and the widow" (v. 9). The mention of "the way of the wicked" in v. 9 recalls Ps 1:6, and the mention of "happy" recalls Ps 1:1. The concluding affirmation of God's reign in v. 10 recalls the enthronement psalms that form the Psalter's theological heart (see chapter 2). These echoes of earlier and strategic portions of the Psalter suggest that Psalm 146 was intentionally placed. That it contains a final occurrence of "happy," followed by a rehearsal of what God wills for and does in the world, seems to be designed as a final, emphatic reminder that true happiness derives from doing God's will. Thus, the Psalter moves to a conclusion by returning to where it began; that is, happiness derives from doing God's will—justice, righteousness, and peace—which we have suggested is the essence of spirituality.

Psalm 1 Today

Even when they cannot quite identify where it comes from, most citizens of the US would say there is a certain ring to the phrase, "The pursuit of happiness." This should be the case, since it comes from one of the country's founding documents, *The Declaration of Independence*. The "pursuit of happiness" is one of those "inalienable rights" with which we have been "endowed by our Creator." The "pursuit of happiness" is a good thing!

But as with any good thing, the "pursuit of happiness" can be misguided and can end up being destructive. Indeed, this is precisely what has happened in recent years, according to psychotherapist and author Mary Pipher. Growing out of her clinical experience and her keen observation of our culture, Pipher discerns what she calls "a crisis of meaning in our culture." She describes it fundamentally as a misguided attempt to pursue happiness:

> We have a crisis of meaning in our culture. The crisis comes from our isolation from each other, from the values we learn in a culture of consumption, and from the fuzzy, self-help message that the only commitment is to the self and the only important question is—Am I happy? We learn that we are number one and that our own immediate needs are the most important ones. The crisis comes from the message that products satisfy and that happiness can be purchased.[2]

A culture that teaches us happiness can be purchased needs help, and it may be that help is on the way. There has emerged in recent years a whole new academic discipline called "happiness studies." It even has its own academic journal, *The Journal of Happiness Studies*. But the academic study of happiness may not ultimately address the crisis. The focus of this new field seems to be upon what people feel or think makes them happy—a certain level of income, satisfactory relationships, the right job or career path, and so on. The possible danger is we will simply have more data to apply to the question that Pipher says is the problem to start with: Am I happy?

The field of happiness studies is new, and perhaps we should give it the benefit of the doubt. But in case it brings us up short, Psalm 1 and the Psalter as a whole are there as an alternative resource. Happiness is not, according to the Psalms, about getting what we want (purchasing it or otherwise) nor about doing what we want. Rather, happiness is about doing what *God* wants—justice, righteousness, and peace. From the perspective of the Psalms, "the pursuit of happiness" is not about *me*. Rather,

2. Pipher, *Shelter of Each Other*, 26.

it is about *us*, including and especially those whose lives are most threatened and vulnerable. In short, "the pursuit of happiness" is fundamentally the pursuit of justice!

Interestingly, although she is working primarily out of a mental-health framework, Mary Pipher commends pursuing happiness in a way that closely resembles the way commended by the Psalms and the Bible as a whole. Note that she mentions the Golden Rule (Matt 7:12) in the following:

> People are at their best and society is strongest when we follow the Golden Rule, which emphasizes caring for self and caring for others. Lives are meaningful and satisfying [that is, happy!] when they involve commitment, justice, truthfulness, and community. . . . Happiness ultimately comes from a sense that one is contributing to the well-being [*shalom*!] of the community. In reality, making wise moral choices is the most direct route to true happiness. . . . The cure for cynicism, depression, and narcissism is social action. Action solves two problems. It makes communities better, and it gives people a sense of meaning and purpose.[3]

Although I am fairly sure that she did not intend it as such, this quote serves as an apt commentary on Psalm 1, which, by way of its sharply drawn contrast between "the way of the righteous" and "the way of the wicked," invites "making wise moral choices." Throughout this volume, it is suggested that authentic spirituality involves action—the pursuit of God's call "to the service of God's righteousness in the world." As it turns out, authentic spirituality may also be the best thing we can do for our own mental health!

Discussion Questions

1. Psalm 1 has often been criticized for being legalistic and for promoting self-righteousness. How would you defend Psalm 1 as an appropriate introduction to the Psalter?

3. Pipher, *Shelter of Each Other*, 126, 159, 251.

2. What does "the pursuit of happiness" mean to you?

3. Do you think we have a "crisis of meaning" in our culture? If so, what is to be done?

4. How might you explain to a friend your understanding of the relationship between justice and happiness?

5

Protesting Injustice

The Psalms of Individual Lament

ONE OF THE MOST remarkable and theologically significant things about the book of Psalms is the pervasive presence of the enemies, both enemies of God and enemies of the righteous pray-ers of the Psalms. They are there in the very first verse of the Psalter, where they are called "the wicked" (Ps 1:1; see also vv. 4, 6), "sinners" (not to be confused with the New Testament notion that everyone is inevitably a sinner), and "scoffers" (that is, those who refuse to attend to God's *torah*, "instruction"; see chapter 4). They are there again in Psalm 2, where they are very explicitly opponents of God as well as opponents of the earthly king, who is responsible for enacting God's will on earth (see Ps 2:2 and chapter 3). And in Psalm 3, the first individual lament (also known as individual complaints or prayers for help as well as protests), the enemies are again very prominent; they immediately make their voices heard (3:1–2):

> O LORD, how many are my foes!
>   Many are rising against me;
> many are saying to me,
>   "There is no help for you in God."

The repetition of "many" emphasizes the extent of the opposition, and the obviously hostile intent of the enemies is made clear by what they say, since what they tell the psalmist directly contradicts the concluding verse of Psalm 2.

Some interpreters consider Psalms 1–3 to be the introduction to the Psalter rather than just Psalm 1 or Psalms 1–2. If this be the case, Psalms 1–3 are appropriately performing their introductory function when they feature the presence of the enemies; for, as it turns out, the enemies are *always* present in the psalms of lament. In fact, Fredrik Lindström concludes that the presence of enemies is the most important interpretive aspect of the psalms of lament. In his words, "The absolutely most important motif in the individual complaint psalms' interpretation of suffering is the *enemy motif* . . . [because] it is found in and throughout the psalms in question."[1] As Lindström suggests, the lament psalms are characterized by two realities. Besides the pervasive presence of the enemy, there is the constant suffering of the psalmists. Indeed, their suffering is precisely what the psalmists are lamenting or complaining about. To be sure, sometimes the psalmists blame God directly for their suffering:

> O LORD, do not rebuke me in your anger,
> or discipline me in your wrath. (Ps 6:1)

> How long, O LORD? Will you forget me forever?
> How long will you hide your face from me? (Ps 13:1)

> My God, my God, why have you forsaken me?
> Why are you so far from helping me,
> from the words of my groaning? (Ps 22:1)

But at other times, the psalmists are clearly aware that their suffering results from the opposition of their enemies:

> O LORD, my God, in you I take refuge;
> save me from all my pursuers, and deliver me,

---

1. Lindström quoted in Brueggemann and Linafelt, *Introduction to the Old Testament*, 323.

> or like a lion they will tear me apart;
>> they will drag me away, with no one to rescue. (Ps 7:1–2)

> Guard me as the apple of the eye,
>> hide me in the shadow of your wings,
> from the wicked who despoil me,
>> my deadly enemies who surround me. (Ps 17:8–9)

At still other times, the psalmists recognize that suffering derives from the enemies, but they blame God indirectly by suggesting that God could and should be doing something to address the situation:

> Why, O LORD, do you stand far off?
>> Why do you hide yourself in times of trouble?
> In arrogance the wicked persecute the poor . . . (Ps 10:1–2a)

But *in every case* (except one—see below), even when they blame God directly or indirectly, the psalmists ultimately affirm that God is *for* the sufferer, not against the sufferer. Consider the subsequent (often the concluding) sections of the psalms that were quoted above:

> The LORD has heard my supplication;
>> the LORD accepts my prayer.
> All my enemies shall be ashamed and struck with terror;
>> they shall turn back, and in a moment be put to shame.
>> (Ps 6:9–10)

> But I trusted in your steadfast love;
>> my heart shall rejoice in your salvation.
> I will sing to the LORD,
>> because he has dealt bountifully with me. (Ps 13:5–6)

> For he [God] did not despise or abhor the affliction
>> of the afflicted;
> he did not hide his face from me,
>> but heard when I cried to him.

From you comes my praise in the great congregation;
my vows I will pay before those who fear him.
The poor shall eat and be satisfied;
those who seek him shall praise the LORD.
May your hearts live forever! (Ps 22:24–26)

Their [the "pursuers" of v. 1 and "the wicked" of v. 9] mischief
returns upon their own heads,
and on their own heads their violence descends.
I will give to the LORD the thanks due to his righteousness;
and sing praises to the name of the LORD, the Most High.
(Ps 7:16–17)

As for me, I shall behold your face in righteousness;
when I awake I shall be satisfied, beholding your likeness.
(Ps 17:15)

O LORD, you will hear the desire of the meek;
you will strengthen their heart, you will incline your ear
to do justice for the orphan and the oppressed,
so that those from earth may strike terror no more.
(Ps 10:17–18)

With the exception of Psalm 88, all the individual laments conclude with something like the above—that is, with celebratory sections that express trust, praise, assurance, or some combination thereof. Earlier generations of scholars called these sections "the certainty of being heard," and there is a great deal of scholarly discussion concerning the reason(s) that the individual laments move from complaint and petition to the rather sudden and somewhat unexpected celebration. Were these sections added later, after the psalmists' requests for help had been answered? Are these sections meant to appease God in view of the rather accusatory things that the psalmists sometimes say? Are these sections meant to be understood as affirmations of faith that God will deliver at some future time?

We do not know for sure. My favorite explanation is a literary-existential one—that is, the effect of juxtaposing complaint and praise, suffering and glory, hurt and hope, in the same poem is to teach us about life in general and the life of faith in particular. As James L. Mays concludes in commenting on Psalm 13, what we learn from the final form of the individual lament psalms, regardless of how they developed, is this: "The agony and the ecstasy belong together as the secret of our identity."[2] In other words, suffering is an inevitable part of human life, including the life of faith.

This in itself is an incredibly important lesson, but more needs to be said. What does it mean that virtually all the individual laments end by locating God *with and for the sufferer, not against the sufferer*? It means, in the first place and perhaps most importantly, that suffering cannot be interpreted as divine punishment (the same lesson emphasized by the book of Job). Indeed, suffering is never something that God inflicts or wills. As we have seen in the previous chapters, God wills justice, righteousness, and peace!

Why suffering then? Some suffering results simply from the fact that human beings are mortal and finite. We do not live forever, and our friends and family members do not live forever. The process of aging can be painful; of course, we also suffer the loss of those whom we love. In this sense, suffering is an inevitable part of human life, and to commit ourselves to faithful, loving connectedness to other mortals will mean that we share their pain. In this sense, suffering is an inevitable part of the life of faith.

But much suffering in the world is a result of *injustice*, and here is where and why the enemies in the Psalms are so important in the interpretive process. Because God is consistently *for and with* the psalmists, God is not to be implicated in the psalmists' suffering. There is someone in the Psalms who is *not* for the psalmists but rather who is consistently aligned *against* them. It is the omnipresent enemies! As we suggested at the beginning of this chapter, the enemies are opponents of God and opponents of the righteous pray-ers of the Psalms. Thus, the individual laments can and should properly be heard as the psalmists' protest against the injustice,

2. Mays, "Psalm 13," 282.

unrighteousness, and oppressive actions of those who oppose God's will and thus inflict suffering on others. And what's more, these psalms can and should still be prayed as protests against injustice and its destructive effects. We turn to an example.

Psalm 5, Then and Now

Given its placement in the Psalter, Psalm 5 is one of the earliest laments. It is the very first psalm to affirm explicitly God's sovereignty when it addresses God as "my King" in v. 2. As we saw in the conclusion to chapter 2, the sovereign of the universe has chosen, for love's sake, not to exercise divine power by sheer force. God exercises power as sheer love, but this means that human beings can choose not to be faithful. And, of course, some do! These are the enemies in the Psalms, and they regularly victimize "the righteous," who suffer at their hands.

The suffering of the psalmist is evident, especially in vv. 1–3, which contain elements of both lament/complaint and request for help. The psalmist's vocabulary indicates the trouble—"my sighing" (v. 1) and "my cry" (v. 2), along with the necessity to "plead my case" (v. 3). That the suffering is inflicted by enemies is evident as well. A variety of words and phrases indicate the extent of the opposition—"The boastful" (v. 5), "evildoers" (v. 5), "the bloodthirsty and deceitful" (v. 6), "my enemies" (v. 8)—as does the description of the hurtful and destructive speech of the opponents (v. 9). Verse 10 makes it clear that the suffering inflicted on the psalmist violates God's will: "They have rebelled against you."

Whereas the enemies create victims, God offers hospitality (v. 7) and help (vv. 8, 11–12). In contrast to the hateful behavior of the enemies, God is motivated by "steadfast love" (v. 7), which is the NRSV translation of *hesed*. "Steadfast love" is a fundamental—perhaps *the* fundamental—attribute of God (see Exod 34:6–7; Pss 86:15; 103:8; 145:8). This is the first occurrence of *hesed* in the Psalter, but it occurs many more times, both as a reason for praising God (see Pss 100:5; 107:1; 117:2; 118:1, 29) as well as the basis for appealing to God for help (see Pss 6:6; 17:7).

As the psalmist affirms, he stands with God in the midst of and despite the opposition of the enemies. Thus, the psalmist is committed to God's loving will, praying to be led in "your righteousness" and "your way" (v. 8). Further indication of the psalmist's faithful stance comes in vv. 11–12, where God's protection is claimed. The word "refuge" is particularly important because it echoes the introductory Psalm 2 (see 2:12). It also anticipates what will become a major theme in the Psalter, particularly in Books I–II, where the individual laments predominate (see 7:1; 11:1; 14:6; 16:1; 25:20; 31:1, 19; 62:7–8).

Furthermore, God stands with the psalmist. Therefore, not only does the psalmist anticipate God's loving welcome (v. 7) but he or she also affirms God's will to "bless the righteous" (v. 12), again in marked contrast to the enemies who victimize them. The pronoun "you" in the final line of the psalm—"you cover them with favor as with a shield" (v. 12)—is emphatic, and the entire line emphasizes that God is *for* the psalmist, not against the psalmist. The verb translated "cover" has royal connotations (see Ps 8:5 where it is translated "crowned"). In short, God, the King (v. 2), wills that human beings be treated royally as well! Because the psalmist is clearly not being treated as God intends people to be treated, Psalm 5 amounts to a sustained protest against the injustice and unrighteousness of the enemies.

Who were the enemies? We do not know. They are never explicitly identified, although their hateful and destructive behavior is clear enough. What has proven to be a problem for the historical-critical study of the Psalms—that is, the inability to identify the enemies—is an advantage to those who pray the Psalms generation after generation. In essence, the enemies in the Psalms are whoever and/or whatever opposes God's will for justice, righteousness, and peace in the world. The open-endedness of the individual laments invites those who pray the Psalms to identify the opponents of God's will in their own time and place.

One striking example of following this invitation is Ernesto Cardenal's *Psalms*. Cardenal was trained in literature but later studied theology, and he was ordained a Roman Catholic priest in his hometown of Granada, Nicaragua, in 1965. He lived through the brutal years of the Somoza dictatorship in Nicaragua, and he was a non-violent supporter of the Sandinista National Liberation Front (FSLN), which succeeded in overthrowing the Somoza regime in 1979 with widespread popular support. He served as Minister of Culture in Nicaragua from July 1979 until 1987.

In his reading and recasting of Psalm 5, Cardenal is not concerned with the question of who the psalmist's enemies *were*. Rather, he is concerned with identifying his enemies and the enemies of the Nicaraguan people, whom the Somozas oppressed and often killed in their over forty years of control (1936–1979). Compare Ps 5:4 and Cardenal's interpretive rereading of it:

> For you are not a God who delights in wickedness;
> evil will not sojourn with you.
> The boastful will not stand before your eyes;
> you hate all evildoers. (Ps 5:4)

> You never plot with dictators
> your politics are straight
> They don't fool you with slick campaigns
> you're not behind them
> the con-men
> the party bosses.[3]

Similarly, compare the description of the speech of the enemies in Ps 5:9–10 with Cardenal's description of the Somoza regime and its violent and death-dealing rhetoric, which he trusts will come to naught:

> For there is no truth in their mouths;
> their hearts are destruction;
> their throats are open graves;
> they flatter with their tongues.
> Make them bear their guilt, O God;
> let them fall by their own counsels;

3. Cardenal, *Psalms*, 39.

because of their many transgressions cast them out,
for they have rebelled against you. (Ps 5:9–10)

Their mouths are machine-guns
and their tongues deal death
Punish them Lord
Make dust of their projects
and cheap ideas
of all their memoranda.[4]

Like the psalmist in 5:11–12, amid opposition and persecution, Cardenal entrusts life and future to God, as the following comparison suggests:

But let all who take refuge in you rejoice;
let them sing for joy.
Spread your protection over them,
so that those who love your name may exult in you.
For you bless the righteous, O LORD;
you cover them with favor as with a shield. (Ps 5:11–12)

When the siren wails the last warning
you will be with me
You will be my refuge
my strength and deep shelter
You will bless the man
who shuns their slogans and campaigns
their hand-outs and all they say
You will circle him with armour
and shield him with all your love.[5]

To be sure, the deplorable situation in Nicaragua when Cardenal composed his *Psalms* may be an extreme example. But unfortunately, as suggested in the introduction, systemic injustice, enforced by overt or covert violence, is still with us in a

4. Cardenal, *Psalms*, 40.
5. Cardenal, *Psalms*, 40.

variety of forms—racism; economic and political arrangements that lead to persistent poverty, hunger, homelessness,[6] and lack of access to education and health care for millions of people (even billions of people) worldwide; and unsustainable patterns of production and consumption that threaten the entire planet. So, Psalm 5 and the other laments beg to be prayed as a step toward identifying and protesting injustice in the world.

The Lament Psalms Today

As we have seen, the prayers in the Psalter are variously known as laments, complaints, prayers for help, and protests. We have highlighted the protest-aspect above, so in concluding this chapter, it may be helpful to highlight another one of these terms—prayers for help—because it makes clear what should be obvious but often is not. In short, the representatives of this type of psalm, which occurs more than any other type in the Psalter, are *prayers*. And in a consideration of spirituality and/or spiritual practices, prayer is traditionally at or near the top of every list. Given the preceding analysis, one might think that these psalms would have played a major part in fostering a spirituality that impels us to pursue the justice, righteousness, and peace that God wills. But such has not been the case. Why?

One reason, as mentioned in the introduction, is people have tended to read the Psalms (and thus to practice spirituality) with a focus on individuals rather than on corporate realities. But beyond this, this type of psalm has generally been ignored in recent years by the church. The prayers for help have often been viewed as negative and off-putting. People seem to prefer more upbeat and positive-sounding songs of praise. We are such good people, we think, that we don't really have enemies. And we're so good at helping ourselves that it may seldom occur to us to ask God

---

6. See Martin, "In the Lectionary," 24. Martin imagines the psalmist's words in Psalm 13 "on the lips of many people living without a home."

for help! All of this is unfortunate or, in the assessment of Walter Brueggemann, "costly."[7]

Brueggemann describes three costs to the loss of lament. First, there is *a psychological cost*—that is, we think it is a sign of weakness to ask for help, so we think we have to pretend that things are fine even when they and/or we are clearly not. Second, there is *a sociological cost*—that is, it is impossible to form and maintain genuine community when people are pretending. Third, and most important for the purposes of this book, there is *a theological cost*. When we fail to pray the prayers for help, we are very apt to forget that God locates Godself on the side of the victimized—that is, God is *for and with* the poor, needy, afflicted, and oppressed rather than the proud, the prosperous, and the powerful (who, of course, are all too willing to claim that "God is on our side"). When we ignore the prayers for help, we miss out on a major impetus toward developing a spirituality that involves the pursuit of justice and righteousness and that forms us to be peacemakers. As Brueggemann puts it, "When the lament form is censured, justice questions cannot be asked and eventually become invisible and illegitimate."[8]

We need to recover what has been and still is in some quarters a tradition of praying the prayers in the Psalter with and for others. Maybe we are not troubled, impoverished, afflicted, discriminated against, oppressed—good! Then we are called to pray the prayers for help as an act of solidarity with those who are, and as a motivation to join God at God's work of establishing justice, setting things right, and making peace. As James L. Mays puts it:

> Could the use of these prayers remind us and bind us to all those in the worldwide church who are suffering in faith and for the faith? . . . There may be no trouble for the present that corresponds to the tribulations described in the psalms. But do we need to do more than call the roll of such places as El Salvador, South Africa, and Palestine to remember that there are sisters

7. Brueggemann, "Costly Loss of Lament," 61–65.
8. Brueggemann, "Costly Loss of Lament," 63–64.

and brothers whose trials could be given voice in our recitation of the psalms? The old church believed that it was all the martyrs who prayed as they prayed the psalmic prayers.[9]

In answer to Mays's questions, *Yes* and *Yes!* The places on the roll call may change from time to time, but undoubtedly, praying the prayers for help will invite us to attend to and protest suffering and injustice in the world. It will impel us to act in solidarity with and for the victims of injustice and oppression. Indeed, such prayer will be an indispensable part of a spirituality of justice-seeking and peacemaking.

Discussion Questions

1. Had you ever noticed the omnipresence of the enemies in the psalms of lament? Why is this important?

2. What, if any, has been your experience with the psalms of lament? Have they been lost? If so, what is the cost, and how might they be recovered?

3. How would you explain to a friend the importance of the psalms of lament in terms of their connection to a spirituality of justice-seeking and peacemaking?

4. The work of Ernesto Cardenal is one example of the use of the psalms of lament in the public square. Can you think of other situations in which the psalms of lament would be especially appropriate and helpful?

9. Mays, *Lord Reigns*, 52.

6

Desperate Pleas for Justice

The Vengeance Psalms

IN THE DISCUSSION OF the prayers in the last chapter, we saw only briefly an element of the psalmic prayers that appears frequently—that is, the psalmists' requests that God obliterate the enemies, or the psalmists' affirmations that God will surely destroy the enemies. The brief exposure to this element in the previous chapter was Ps 5:10:

> Make them bear their guilt, O God;
>> let them fall by their own counsels;
>> because of their many transgressions cast them out,
>>> for they have rebelled against you.

This verse contains petitions addressed to God against the enemies. Sometimes, a similar sentiment is expressed as an affirmation, and this element occurs as early as the first prayer for help in the Psalter:

> For you strike all my enemies on the cheek;
>> you break the teeth of the wicked. (Ps 3:7b)

Such expressions of vengeance occur in one or the other of its forms—that is, either a petition or an affirmation—in fifty-nine psalms! This reality is not really surprising, however, given the omnipresence of the enemies that we noted in the previous chapter. Its prevalence almost certainly helps to account for the fact that the church has largely ignored the prayers for help (see chapter 5)—that is, this sentiment has sounded decidedly "un-Christian." Christians are supposed to forgive, and Jesus commanded his disciples to love their enemies rather than asking God to punish or obliterate them!

The problem is compounded by the fact that the psalmists' requests that God dispose of their enemies become the dominant element in several psalms, which have become variously known as imprecatory psalms, cursing psalms, vengeance psalms, or psalms of divine wrath. The lists of these psalms vary from commentator to commentator, but one recent study suggests the following: Psalms 12, 44, 58, 83, 109, 137, and 139.[1] It is not necessary to examine all of these psalms in order to assess their significance for a spirituality of justice-seeking and peacemaking. We shall look in detail at two of them, beginning with one of the more dramatic examples, and I shall suggest that these psalms are not as "un-Christian" as they first may sound.

Psalm 109

Not surprisingly, the enemies are immediately in view (vv. 2–5). As in Ps 5:6, 8, and frequently in the Psalms, the speech of the enemies is "deceitful" (v. 2) and destructive. The psalmist describes his or her behavior toward others as "my love" (vv. 4–5), but it is met only with "words of hate" (v. 3) and "hatred for my love" (v. 5). The enemies "attack" (v. 3) and "accuse" (v. 4; see vv. 20, 25, 29). It is crucial that we realize that the psalmist has been victimized—cruelly attacked and unjustly accused.

To be sure, the psalmist does not "turn the other" cheek (Matt 5:39) but instead launches into an extended, vitriolic speech, which is directed to God, and which has aptly been described

---

1. Zenger, *God of Vengeance?*, 25–61.

as a "song of hate" (vv. 6–19).[2] The speech is so thorough in its wish for the enemies' demise (including their children, all their posterity, as well as any memory of them) that the NRSV translators did not want to assign this "song of hate" to the psalmist. So, they added "They say" to introduce v. 6, thus assigning the speech to the enemies. This is unnecessary. The psalmists are perfectly capable of this sort of sentiment and discourse, even if this is an extreme case. And even if one goes in the interpretive direction of the NRSV, it does not really let the psalmist off the hook. In v. 20, the psalmist claims the preceding speech, even if it were uttered originally by the enemies!

But before we label the psalmist's behavior and speech as "un-Christian," we need to think more carefully. The psalmist has been severely victimized, and the absolute worst thing to tell victims is to "stay silent" and "keep it to yourself." To allow the psalmists their outbursts is simply good pastoral care! Furthermore, the psalmist verbalizes *feelings* of retaliation; the psalmist does *not* actually retaliate. In other words, insofar as revenge is concerned, the psalmist *prays* the vengeful feelings, thereby offering them to God.[3] Thus, the cycle of violence is broken. Perhaps the psalmist is less "un-Christian" than we might think.

It is interesting that the keyword in Psalm 109, which features this extended "song of hate," is "steadfast love" (the single word *hesed* in Hebrew; see above on Psalm 5 in chapter 5). The appearance of this word is evident in vv. 21, 26, and as in Psalm 5, it is the basis for the psalmist's appeal for divine help. But the word occurs twice more—vv. 12 and 16—where it is translated as "kindness." As v. 16 makes clear, the real problem with the enemies is their failure to love: "For he did not remember to show kindness, but pursued the poor and needy and the brokenhearted to their death." This failure has destructive and potentially deadly consequences (see also v. 31), not for the enemies themselves but rather for their victims, which include the psalmist.

---

2. Brueggemann, *Message of the Psalms*, 83. See also Firth, *Surrendering Retribution*.

3. See Firth, *Surrendering Retribution*.

The behavior of the enemies is particularly egregious because it involves taking advantage of the "poor and needy" (vv. 16, 22). As we saw in chapter 1, Psalm 82 affirms that God has particular concern for the poor and needy; indeed, the essence of divinity is to attend to, provide for, and empower those whose lives are threatened and vulnerable. Such is also the essence of justice, the keyword in Psalm 82, and righteousness, which are the foundations of the peace that God intends. Appropriately, therefore, Psalm 109 concludes by locating God "at the right hand of the needy" (v. 31). The psalmist's vengeful-sounding outburst in Psalm 109, along with similar expressions elsewhere in the Psalms, is not simply a matter of personal revenge. Rather, it is a matter of justice. In the final analysis, then, Psalm 109 and the other vengeance psalms are prayers for justice. They desperately express the fervent desire that God set things right for the poor, the needy, and victims of injustice and oppression anywhere. One more example will suffice.

Psalm 12

As in Psalm 109, the other vengeance psalms, and the prayers for help in general, the enemies are present and prominent. In this case, things seem so unbearably out of control that the psalmist begins and ends the psalm with a particularly discouraging assessment of the situation:

> Help, O LORD, for there is no longer anyone who is godly,
> the faithful have disappeared from humankind. (Ps 12:1)

> On every side the wicked prowl,
> as vileness is exalted among humankind. (Ps 12:8)

As in Psalms 5 and 109 and many of the prayers for help, the speech of the enemies is deceitful and destructive (vv. 2–4). As in Psalm 3, the enemies are quoted, and their words reveal their self-centeredness and their desire to demean and dominate others:

> "With our tongues we will prevail;
>   our lips are our own—who is our master?" (Ps 12:4)

The subsequent verse reveals the destructive effects of the enemies' behavior—as in Psalm 109, "the poor are despoiled" and "the needy groan" (v. 5). It is the desperate situation of the poor and needy that motivates the psalmist to pray for God to deal with the enemies:

> May the LORD cut off all flattering lips,
>   the tongue that makes great boasts. . . . (Ps 12:3)

And it is the plight of the poor and needy that impels God to say:

> "I will now rise up," says the LORD,
>   "I will place them in the safety for which they long."
>   (Ps 12:5)

As in Psalm 109 and the other vengeance psalms, the real issue is not personal revenge. Rather, the issue is injustice that threatens the well-being and the very lives of the poor and needy. Again, these prayers are fundamentally prayers by justice-seekers.

The Vengeance Psalms Today

The final line of Psalm 12 sounds like a perfect description of what is happening today, at least in the United States: "Vileness is exalted among humankind." Political advertising and political discourse in general have devolved into "lies" (v. 2), "flattering lips" (vv. 2–3), and "great boasts" (v. 3) that reveal a nearly total absorption with the self and a desire to dominate others for personal gain—"who is our master?" Increasingly, the result is that "the poor are despoiled" and "the needy groan," as the gap between the impoverished and the super-rich continues to grow, as millions struggle for access to health insurance and care, as low-wage workers clamor for a living wage, as the prison-industrial complex capitalizes upon the discovery that money can be made by locking up more people, and so on! One cannot help but wonder what has happened to the formerly cherished notion of "the general welfare" or "the common good," either of which might be an appropriate and helpful translation of *shalom*. It seems that "the faithful have disappeared from humankind," or at least from the leadership of the country.

For this reason, the vengeance psalms may be particularly important at this moment in our history. They are an invitation to identify victimization and injustice; they provide examples of letting victims speak; and they are essentially prayers for justice. As Erich Zenger concludes concerning these psalms:

> These are poetic prayers that hold up a mirror to the *perpetrators* of violence, and they are prayers that can help the *victims* of violence, by placing on their lips a cry for justice, . . . [by urging them] to hold fast to their human dignity and to endure *nonviolently*, in prayerful protest against a violence that is repugnant to God, despite their fear in the face of their enemies and the images of enmity.[4]

As prayers for justice that invite and facilitate the implementation of the justice, righteousness, and peace that God wills, especially for the vulnerable and victimized, these prayers are anything but "un-Christian." Indeed, if one listens closely, one will hear an anticipation of the prayer that Jesus taught his disciples: "Your kingdom come, your will be done, on earth as it is in heaven" (Matt 6:10).

Discussion Questions

1. The vengeance psalms are probably the ones that bother people the most. How would you explain to a friend that these psalms are anything but "un-Christian"?

2. Why is it important to let victims speak? How are victims silenced in our society?

3. Violence in the US has reached epidemic proportions. How might the vengeance psalms promote non-violence?

4. Zenger, *God of Vengeance?*, 92.

7

Celebrating Justice

The Songs of Praise

WE HAVE ACTUALLY ALREADY seen the connection between praise and justice because the enthronement psalms (see chapter 2) are songs of praise (sometimes also known as hymns). But there is more to be said. In this chapter, we shall see that the celebration of justice is not confined to the enthronement psalms. It is also explicit in songs of praise and hymnic material elsewhere in the Psalter. Even where justice and righteousness are not explicitly mentioned, praise itself invites submission to God and thus the pursuit of God's will for the world—the pursuit of justice, righteousness, and peace that is at the heart of spirituality.

Psalm 33

Psalm 33 stands out in Book I of the Psalter (Psalms 1–41), not only because it is one of the few songs of praise in Book I but also because it is the only psalm in Book I—aside from Psalms 1 and 2—that does not have a superscription. In fact, the opening verse of Psalm 33 seems to suggest that this psalm is a continuation of Psalm 32, since it echoes the invitation to praise with which Psalm 32 concludes.

Be that as it may, Psalm 33 now stands independently as a song of praise, and its first five verses demonstrate the simple, typical structure of this type of psalm. The five invitations to praise—"Rejoice in the LORD" (v. 1), "Praise the LORD" (v. 2), "make melody" (v. 2), "Sing . . . a new song" (v. 3; see Pss 96:1; 98:1), and "play skillfully" (v. 3)—are followed by reasons for praise, introduced here, as is often the case, by the conjunction "for" (v. 4).

It is these reasons for praise that are particularly noteworthy. Verse 4 mentions both God's "word" and God's "work," and the simple juxtaposition of vv. 4 and 5 is significant. Verse 5 reads:

> He [God] loves righteousness and justice;
> the earth is full of the steadfast love of the LORD.

In short, the juxtaposition of vv. 4 and 5 suggests that the concrete content of both God's "word" and God's "work" is justice and righteousness! And as v. 5 itself indicates, it is precisely God's will for and work toward justice and righteousness that is evidence of God's world-encompassing "steadfast love" (Hebrew *hesed*). As it turns out, "steadfast love" becomes the keyword of Psalm 33, occurring again in vv. 18 and 22. And the expansive perspective of v. 5 continues throughout the psalm—see "all the earth" and "all the inhabitants of the world" (v. 5); "all humankind" (v. 13); and "all the inhabitants of the earth" (v. 14). We also saw such expansiveness in Psalms 96 and 98, along with Psalm 82 (see chapters 1–2); it is typical for the songs of praise (see the invitations to praise in Pss 66:1, 8; 67:3–5, 7; 100:1; 117:1; 148:1–12; 150:6). In short, God loves the world, the whole world, and "all the inhabitants" (vv. 5, 14) therein (see Ps 24:1 and below on Psalm 104). This explains, of course, why God also "loves righteousness and justice" (Ps 33:5).

A Note on Psalm 36

Psalm 36 is usually categorized as a lament because of vv. 1–4, which describe "the wicked" (v. 1), and because of vv. 11–12, which ask for and envision deliverance from "the wicked" (v. 11; see chapters 5 and 6). But the laments and other types of psalms regularly contain hymnic elements. In the case of Psalm 36, vv. 5–10 offer a lovely rehearsal of reasons for praising God. As in Psalm 33, the thematic keyword in Ps 36:5–10 is "steadfast love" (vv. 5, 7, 10); vv. 5–6 are very reminiscent of Ps 33:5, which affirms that "the earth is full of the steadfast love of the LORD." Psalm 36:5–6 offers a more extensive and expansive poetic portrayal of this affirmation, and again, like Ps 33:5, Ps 36:5–6 associates God's justice and righteousness with God's steadfast love:

> Your steadfast love, O LORD, reaches the heavens,
>   your faithfulness to the clouds.
> Your righteousness is like the mighty mountains,
>   your acts of justice like the great deep;
>   you save humans and animals, O LORD. (my translation)

"Steadfast love" and "faithfulness" comprise a shorthand summary of the essence of God's character (see Exod 34:6; Pss 86:15; 89:14; 100:5; 117:2), and as we have seen from the outset, righteousness and justice summarize God's will for the world. Notice the downward spatial movement of these elements—from heavens to clouds to mountaintops to sea level and below. In short, according to the psalmist's poetic vision, God's character and will pervade the universe!

The result is articulated by the final line of v. 6. In biblical terms, "salvation" means life as God intends it to be; God intends that the universe support life for both human beings and the other creatures. Not surprisingly, the subsequent verses describe what it takes for life to thrive—protection (v. 7, "refuge in the shadow of your wings") along with food and drink that God provides (v. 8). The drink comes "from the river of your delights," and the Hebrew word underlying "delights" is a noun that elsewhere is the proper noun "Eden" (see Gen 2:8, 10, 15), thus recalling stories of the creation of life in the opening chapters of Genesis. Verse 9 reinforces the conclusion that the fundamental issue is life: "For with you is the fountain of life." God's protecting, nurturing, and loving purpose and work are intended for "All people" (v. 7) as well as for all creatures (again, see below on Psalm 104).

Such is the essence of justice and righteousness, which is to be celebrated, and for which God is to be praised. The same message comes through clearly in Psalm 103.

Psalm 103

The invitation to praise in Ps 103:1–2 is unusual because the psalmist invites his or her own self to praise God: "Bless the LORD, my whole being" (vv. 1–2, CEB; see also v. 22; Pss 104:1, 35; 146:1). Following the invitation to praise in vv. 1–2, a series of participles in vv. 3–5 articulate the reasons for praise as they elaborate upon God's "benefits"—"who forgives" (v. 3), "who heals" (v. 3), "who redeems" (v. 4), "who crowns" (v. 4), "who satisfies" (v. 5). All of these divine activities are in the service of life as God intends life to be; they range from the routine provision of food ("who satisfies you with good," v. 5) to life-saving intervention in the face of deadly threat ("who redeems your life from the Pit," v. 4; "the Pit" is another name for Sheol, the realm of the dead).

Although the NRSV and other major translations obscure it (by leaving a space after v. 5), the series of participles actually continues into v. 6. In fairness to the translators, the Hebrew syntax is altered slightly in v. 6 since the participle, "(the one who) works," is provided with a subject—"the LORD." Even so, the continuation of the participial series suggests that v. 6 is the culmination and perhaps the summarizing conclusion of all the preceding verses:

> (It is the) LORD who works righteousness
>   and justice for all who are oppressed. (my translation)

If this be the case, and I think it is, then it is not surprising that God's "benefits" are summed up by the terms "righteousness" (NRSV "vindication") and "justice." In short, it is the case again, as with Psalms 33 and 36, that Psalm 103 features God's justice and righteousness, for which God is to be praised. Like Psalms 33 as well as 36, Psalm 103 also highlights God's "steadfast love." The word *hesed* occurs in vv. 4, 8, 11, and 17. In v. 4, it follows immediately after the affirmation that God restores life. In the context of vv. 3–6, the implication is that God's will for and work toward justice and righteousness are motivated essentially by God's love. Here again is reason for God to be praised.

At first glance, it may seem that Psalm 103 lacks the expansiveness that generally characterizes the songs of praise, since the psalmist invites his or her own self to praise God. But already in v. 6, the psalmist affirms that God's will for and work toward justice and righteousness are "for all who are oppressed"—that is, for all whose lives are threatened in any way. This category would include *everyone* at some point, so it is not surprising that a psalm that begins with a focus on the individual psalmist concludes with a universal perspective, including several more occurrences of the word "all." Before the opening invitation, "Bless the LORD, my whole being," recurs in v. 22 to conclude Psalm 103, it is accompanied by a similar invitation to "Bless the LORD" that is addressed to God's "messengers" (v. 20, my translation; NRSV "angels"), "mighty ones" (v. 20), "all his hosts" (v. 21), "his ministers" (v. 21), and "all his works, in all places of his dominion" (v. 22). That the psalmist is to join his or her individual voice with a universal chorus of praise suggests finally that God's will for and work toward justice and righteousness are nothing short of creation-encompassing. Not coincidentally, in this regard, the invitation to "Bless the LORD, my whole being" also encompasses Psalm 104 (vv. 1, 35), a psalm that has the whole creation in view.

Psalm 104

The shared invitation to praise that opens and concludes Psalms 103 and 104, "Bless the LORD, my whole being" (Pss 103:1, 22; 104:1, 35) clearly indicates that these two psalms were intended to be read and heard together. As we have seen, Psalm 103 begins with a focus on an individual, and it concludes with an invitation to bless that is addressed to "all his works, in all places of his dominion" (v. 22). This conclusion anticipates admirably the content of Psalm 104 and its portrayal of the variety and extent of God's "works." The Hebrew root underlying "works" in 103:22 becomes the keyword in Psalm 104 (see "make[s]"/"made" in 104:4, 19, 24b and "work[s]" in 104:13, 24a, 31).

Verses 2–3 introduce the first of God's manifold works. The language includes several architectural terms—"tent" (v. 2), "beams" (v. 3), and "chambers" (v. 3). The word "tent" occurs most often in the account of the building of the wilderness tabernacle (see Exod 26:2 where the word occurs three times; NRSV "curtain[s]"). While the tabernacle was God's temporary dwelling in the wilderness, Psalm 104 suggests that ultimately God resides in the creation itself:

> You stretch out the heavens like a tent,
> > you set the beams of your chambers on the waters, . . .
> (vv. 2b-3a)

God's home is the entire universe!

The focus on God's works in the heavenly realm (vv. 2b–4; see "made" in v. 4) gives way to a focus on "the earth," whose "foundations" are such that "it shall never be shaken" (v. 5). Psalm 104 does not contain the words "justice" or "righteousness," but this verse is reminiscent of other psalms that do. Recall Psalm 82, in which the keyword is "justice" (see chapter 1). In Ps 82:5, "all the foundations of the earth are shaken" because of the lack of the justice that God wills. And recall Psalm 96, where in v. 10 the firmly established world "shall never be moved" (NRSV; the underlying Hebrew of "moved" is the same root translated "shaken" in Pss 82:5 and 104:5). Why? Because God "has come to establish justice" (v. 12, my translation; see chapter 2), good news that is greeted by a creation-wide community (vv. 11–12) much like the one described in Psalm 104. Considering these three texts together—Psalms 82, 96, and 104— we can conclude that the creation of a life-sustaining world is an act of divine justice, for which God is to be praised.

The focus on the earth continues through v. 13, and then vv. 14–23 enumerate the inhabitants of the earth. Yes, this includes people (vv. 14, 23), but far more—cattle (v. 14), plants (v. 14), the "trees of the LORD" (v. 16; and note well that Psalm 104 does *not* include the much more frequent phrase, "people of the LORD"!), birds (v. 17), wild goats (v. 18), coneys (v. 18; see the NIV note, "rock badgers"), "all the animals of the forest" (v. 20), "young lions" (v. 21), and perhaps the moon and sun (v. 19) should also be considered inhabitants, or at least vital parts of the community of creation. In any case, v. 24 has all of the above in view as the psalmist exuberantly exclaims, "O LORD, how manifold are your works! In wisdom you have made them all; the earth is full of your creatures" (or "your creations," according to the CEB).

As Psalm 104 moves toward a conclusion, more creatures are named—"creeping things" that fill the sea (v. 25) and even Leviathan (v. 26; see Ps 74:14; Job 41:1–34), the mythic chaos monster that here has been reduced to a plaything (v. 26b; my translation of this line is, "and Leviathan that you formed to play with him"). All God's creatures, human and non-human, are provided for, including the daily necessity of food (vv. 27–28) and the second-by-second necessity of air to breathe (vv. 29–30). The implication of v. 30b is that every breath the creatures take is, in some sense, an act of new creation, serving to renew "the face of the ground."

The psalmist's final reflections (vv. 31–34) are framed by joy. The psalmist wishes that "the LORD rejoice in his works" (v. 31; this is the final of the six occurrences of the keyword "works"), and the psalmist affirms, "I rejoice in the LORD" (v. 34). This shared joy is important, for it suggests that not only is God to be praised for God's creative and life-sustaining work but also that the psalmist is committed, for God's sake (literally!), to the care of the creation that God enjoys. It might be anachronistic to say that the psalmist was an environmentalist; however, as James L. Mays concludes, the psalmist "is informed by a basic ecological sense of the interdependence of things."[1]

Actually, there is one more verse following vv. 31–34. The first two lines of v. 35 are omitted by the Revised Common Lectionary, presumably because they seem to introduce an unpleasant note into the psalmist's joyful song of praise (see v. 33). But we

---

1. Mays, *Psalms*, 334. For more on Psalm 104 and how the Psalms as a whole are a resource for an ecological spirituality, see Walker-Jones, *Green Psalter*; the treatment of Psalm 104 is on pp. 139–42.

need to hear these two lines because they express the fervent desire that no one disrupt the intricate, interdependent, life-serving, and joy-inspiring creation that derives from and belongs to God. In this era of human-caused ecological threat and degradation, we need to hear these lines because *we* are the wicked! Setting his- or herself in sharp contrast to the wicked, the psalmist repeats the opening line of the psalm, "Bless the LORD, my whole being." In short, the psalmist commands the self to submit to God and to commit to joining God in the joyful work of sustaining the life of the world. And appropriately, there is one more word (in Hebrew)—*Hallelujah!* "Praise the LORD!" As Mays observes, "The psalm concludes with the first Hallelujah found in the Psalter. Could a more appropriate place be found"?[2]

The Songs of Praise for Today

The invitation "Bless the LORD" is noteworthy. In some sense, it is virtually synonymous with the more frequent hymnic invitation, "Praise the LORD." But "bless" in Psalms 103–4 and elsewhere (see Pss 16:7; 34:1; 64:4; 100:4; 115:18; 134:1–2; 135:18–20; 145:2, 10) represents a Hebrew root that has the more specific connotation of "kneel." (There is a Hebrew noun formed from this root that means "knees.") In short, to "bless the LORD" implies submission to God, and thus submission to God's word and God's work—that is, to bless the LORD means to pursue the justice, righteousness, and peace that God intends for humankind and for the whole creation.

As suggested from the outset (see the introduction and chapter 1), the needs of the human family are staggering—poverty, hunger, homelessness, racism, displacement, discrimination, epidemic violence, warfare, and more. And in this frightening era of rapid global warming, extreme climate change, and out-of-control wildfires and storms, the alarming rate of the disappearance of plant and animal species, and more, the needs of the earth are also paramount. As Bill McKibben concludes, "This

2. Mays, *Psalms*, 336.

environmental devastation stands as the single great crisis of our time, surpassing and encompassing all others."[3] As Pope Francis reminds us, justice for the human community is inseparable from justice for the earth. Although it may sound simplistic and naïve, Pope Francis has also suggested that praise is where solutions to our crises begin.[4]

The nuance of meaning of the word "bless" helps to clarify for us the meaning of "praise." Praise—while it is an important liturgical activity that involves music, singing, testimony, clapping, and dancing (see Pss 33:2–3; 47:1, 6; 66:4; 67:4; 108:1–3; 135:3; 138:5; 145:7, 21; 147:1; 149:1–3; 150:3–6)—cannot be confined to liturgy. Praise is also, as Claus Westermann once put it, a "mode of existence."[5] Or, we might say, praise is both liturgy and lifestyle. Worship should orient us to discern God's character and will for the world; it should also equip us to submit to God and to commit ourselves to the pursuit of justice, righteousness, and peace.

When worship fails to orient us to discern God's will and to join God at God's work in the world—that is, when there is a disconnect between praise as liturgy and praise as lifestyle—then worship becomes unacceptable, indeed offensive, to God. This is why the prophets regularly criticized Israelite and Judean worship, calling leaders and people back to the pursuit of justice and righteousness. The prophet Isaiah, for instance, says that God "hates" the occasions on which the people of Judah gathered for worship (Isa 1:14). What God desires is this:

> learn how to do good;
> seek justice; set victimizers straight;
> establish justice for the orphan; be an advocate for the widow.
> (Isa 1:17, my translation)

And in perhaps the most famous criticism of worship, the prophet Amos says this:

---

3. McKibben, *Comforting Whirlwind*, 15.

4. Francis, *Laudato Si' [Praise Be to You]*, 1 (paragraph 1), 76–77 (paragraphs 156–58). See also Boff, *Cry of the Earth, Cry of the Poor*, xi.

5. Westermann, *Praise and Lament in the Psalms*, 159.

I hate, I despise your festivals,
and I take no delight in your solemn assemblies. . . .
Take away from me the noise of your songs;
I will not listen to the melody of your harps.
But let justice roll down like waters,
and righteousness like an ever-flowing stream.
(Amos 5:21, 23–24; see also Isa 58:6–7; Jer 7:1–7; Hos 6:6; Mic
6:6–8: Pss 50:23; 51:16–17)

According to the prophets, the people may be gathered; the harpists may be playing; the people may be singing; but it will not truly be praise unless the liturgy facilitates a lifestyle focused on justice and righteousness, defined exactly as Psalm 82 laid it out—attention to and provision for the vulnerable and the victimized. And as we have seen, Psalm 104 expands that vision to include attention to and provision for the life of the whole creation. In this chapter, we have seen how the language and activity of praise is explicitly associated with justice and righteousness in Psalms 33, 36, and 103. But even when the words "justice" and "righteousness" are not present, as is the case with Psalm 104, the invitation to praise itself invites submission to God and the pursuit of God's will for the world—justice, righteousness, and peace. It was true in ancient Israel and Judah, and it is still true today. It was then, and is now, at the essence of spirituality.

Discussion Questions

1. What is your definition of praise? Had it ever occurred to you that praise is related to justice-seeking and peacemaking?

2. In your opinion, how should liturgy and lifestyle be related?

3. The "noise of your songs" in Amos 5:23 almost certainly refers to the use of the Psalms in ancient Israel. How do the prophets help us understand the songs of praise?

4. A case can be made that ecological responsibility begins with praising God. What do you think?

8

"In Paths of Righteousness"

Psalm 23 as a Call to Justice

IN OUR JOURNEY THROUGH the Psalter with the goal of reading or rereading the traditional psalm-types through the lens of God's commitment to justice, righteousness, and peace, it might seem that we arrive at a roadblock when we come to the psalms of assurance, the most outstanding example of which is Psalm 23. Psalm 23 is, after all, a "funeral psalm," or at least so we think. Or, if it is not a funeral psalm, it is one for use at the bedside of those who are critically ill or in other situations of extremity, threat, or distress.

To be sure, Psalm 23 functions powerfully in settings of loss and grief as well as in situations that confront us with threats of various kinds. But this reality does not exhaust the potential meaning and usefulness of Psalm 23. Philip Jenkins, a student of the global church, reports, for instance, that in certain contexts, Psalm 23 functions effectively and powerfully as "a political tract."[1] Christians who live under oppressive regimes in Africa and Asia point an accusing finger at a tyrant, while they say, "The LORD is my shepherd, and *you are not!*" While it would never occur to

1. Jenkins, "Liberating Word," 26.

66

Christians in the US to view Psalm 23 as "a political tract," its use elsewhere in this manner is a clue to how even Psalm 23 articulates God's will for justice, righteousness, and peace. As such, it is at least an implicit invitation to follow God's leading, to join God at God's work in the world, which is the essence of spirituality.

Psalm 23 and Ezekiel 34:1–16

By far the biblical text that is most akin to Psalm 23 is Ezek 34:1–16, a text that makes clear the political dimension of the term "shepherd." In the ancient Near East, the term "shepherd" could refer not only to the humble folk who watched out for sheep but also to the most exalted folk in the ancient cultural context—kings. With this in mind, we note in Ezek 34:2 that the prophet is called to prophesy "to the shepherds"—that is to the kings and the royal bureaucracy. The divine complaint against the shepherds/kings is that they are not doing what Psalm 72 says they are supposed to do. As we saw in chapter 3, the fundamental responsibility of the king was to attend to and care for the people, beginning with the poor, needy, and most vulnerable, and this task started with providing food. Indeed, "shepherd" in Hebrew literally means "one who feeds." But in Ezekiel 34, the shepherds are addressed and described as those who "have been feeding yourselves . . . but you do not feed the sheep" (Ezek 34:3). Neither have the shepherds attended to nor provided for the most vulnerable—"the weak . . . the sick . . . the strayed . . . the lost" (v. 4). Instead, "with force and harshness you have ruled them" (v. 4), and the result is that the sheep "were scattered over the face of the earth" (v. 6).

Because the shepherds/kings have failed miserably to feed, provide for, and protect their flock, they are judged. God says that God will take over the shepherd-role: "I myself will search for my sheep, and will seek them out" (v. 11); "I will rescue them" (v. 12); "I will feed them on the mountains of Israel" (v. 13; see above on the significance of mountains in Ps 72:3 in chapter 3); "I will seek the lost" (v. 16); "I will bind up the injured" (v. 16); "I will strengthen the weak" (v. 16). In short, God says, "I myself will be the shepherd of the sheep" (v. 15). The concluding summary statement is this: "I will feed them with justice" (v. 16). As we learned from Psalm 72, justice is exactly what the kings were supposed to do, along with righteousness, toward the accomplishment of peace, because it was their job to enact and embody God's will (see chapters 1–3).

It is to be noted that what God says that God will do in Ezekiel 34—summarized by the word "justice"—is exactly what God does in Psalm 23. God meets every need so that the sheep "lack nothing" (v. 1, CEB). It starts with the provision of food—that is, the sheep "lie down in green pastures" (v. 2), which for sheep means a place to eat. Food is accompanied by another and even more basic necessity—that is, water. It is provided by the "still waters" (v. 2), which are required for sheep to be able to drink, since they are frightened by a current or flowing stream. Food and water are the basic necessities of life, and that is the point here. God wills and provides for life, as the next phrase in Psalm 23 affirms. Better than the traditional "he restores my soul" is the translation, "he keeps me alive" (v. 3, CEB).

The basic provisions for life are accompanied by protection—that is, being led in "right paths," which for a sheep can clearly mean the difference between life and death. While "right paths" fits the shepherd-sheep metaphor better than the traditional "paths of righteousness," the latter is a reminder that the metaphor is intended to put us in touch with God's will for people, not just sheep. As we have seen, "righteousness" is virtually synonymous with "justice," and the two words are often paired. It is fitting, therefore, that Ezekiel 34 summarizes God's provision and protection with the word "justice," while the concluding observation about God's provision and protection in Psalm 23 employs the word "righteousness." This providing and protecting is "for his name's sake," which means that this is just the way God is. In short, it is God's fundamental character to will and work for life; or, as suggested in chapter 1 on the basis of Psalm 82, a key part of what it means to be God is to provide for the needs of people, beginning with the most threatened and vulnerable.

It is v. 4 that relates most directly to the traditional use of Psalm 23 in the United States. God's protection continues, but now God's presence and protection come in "the darkest valley" or "the valley of the shadow of death" (RSV). The phrase, in either translation, suggests a threat of some kind, perhaps even a deadly threat, the kind of situation we ordinarily think about when we consider Psalm 23. In keeping with the tone of vv. 1–3, however, v. 5 returns to a setting that again involves God's routine daily provision for life. While the metaphor has shifted from shepherd to host, the same elements of provision and protection are involved. The "table before me" represents food; the overflowing cup represents drink; and the anointing with oil indicates safety and security.

Just as vv. 1–3 concluded by alluding to God's character, so v. 6 employs the one word in the Old Testament that best describes God's character, and it is a word that we have seen before. It is *hesed*, although the NRSV translates it here as "mercy" instead of its usual "steadfast love." In short, God provides for and protects life because God loves! The affirmation is stronger than the traditional translations suggest. The verb usually translated "shall follow" really means "shall *pursue*." God's goodness and love are in active pursuit of the psalmist, which explains why God is portrayed as providing and protecting, both on a daily basis and in situations of threat and extremity. In a word, this is *justice*, as the Bible defines it. In two words, this is *justice and righteousness*, both motivated by divine love.

Those Omnipresent Enemies Again

As we saw in chapter 5, the enemies are always present in the laments. But here they are again in Psalm 23, which is a psalm of assurance. Why are they here, and what are they doing in Ps 23:5? The answer to this question is unclear. What is clear is that the enemies are not a threat as they always are in the laments. The occurrence of the word "shall pursue" is telling in this regard. Elsewhere in the Psalms, it is the enemies who regularly *pursue* the psalmists. In Psalm 23, there is a pursuit, but it is God's goodness and steadfast love that are doing the pursuing. This is a best-case scenario, and this is the fundamental assurance that Psalm 23 offers.

It is still not clear what the enemies are doing in v. 5. Some interpreters like to think that the psalmist, while sitting at the table and eating, taunts the enemies between bites—that is, the enemies are not at the table. This construal may be correct; we simply do not know for sure. But this conclusion seems to me unnecessarily negative, hostile, and exclusivistic. Is it not possible, I wonder, to imagine that the enemies are at the table, sharing the meal with the psalmist? If the immediate literary context is taken into account, such a situation is not so difficult to imagine. Psalm 22, like Psalm 23, ends with a meal. The mention of vows in Ps 22:25 and eating in Ps 22:26 seems to indicate that the psalmist has in mind a thanksgiving sacrifice, which ordinarily would have involved both the psalmist and the psalmist's guests consuming a portion of the sacrificial animal. But this is no ordinary sacrificial meal! In the psalmist's hyperbolic portrayal of this meal, *everyone* is invited—"All the ends of the earth," "all the families of the nations" (v. 27), and even the dead (v. 29) and future generations (vv. 30–31). If the expansive perspective of Ps 22:25–31 carries over into Psalm 23, then it is easy to picture the enemies at the table with the psalmist in Ps 23:5. They, too, are fed! And, of course, Psalm 23 is followed by a psalm that shares the expansive perspective of the conclusion of Psalm 22:

> The earth is the LORD's and all that is in it,
> the world, and those who live in it. (Ps 24:1)

If all people belong to God, then whom would God not want to feed?

If this interpretive direction is followed, then the expansiveness we saw in the songs of praise and Psalm 82 (see chapters 1 and 7) is also present in Psalm 23. Indeed, the ultimate assurance involves not just the neutralization of nor escape from our enemies, but rather reconciliation with our enemies, a possibility that may start with envisioning a table at which everyone is fed.

Psalm 23 for Today

Psalm 23 will undoubtedly continue to function powerfully in situations of loss, grief, distress, and threat, as it should. My concern in this chapter is not to question this dimension of meaning and use of Psalm 23, but rather to suggest that this dimension need not be the only one. The psalmist celebrates God's providing and protecting presence *every day* (see v. 6), not just in times of extremity or threat. In short, the psalmist affirms that life, along with everything that sustains life, is a divine gift, not just a human accomplishment.

Such an affirmation is a radical faith-stance in our culture of merit and "deserving it." We are so oriented to achieve that it is very difficult for us to receive life as a gift. If we can open ourselves to God's gift of life, our fundamental posture will be gratitude. As Elsa Tamez points out, only people who live with gratitude will be inclined to share their gifts and resources with others; or, as she puts it, grace and gratitude result in solidarity.[2] Such solidarity—the sharing of gifts and resources with and for all—is the foundation for the justice, righteousness, and peace that God intends. As we have seen, God's justice and righteousness involve not giving people what they deserve, but rather giving people what they need. This is precisely what the shepherd does in Psalm 23. To live in the presence of this shepherd (Ps 23:4), to be at home with this gracious host (Ps 23:5–6), is to be led in paths of righteousness (Ps 23:3) and to be seated at a table where everyone is able to eat (23:5).

Discussion Questions

1. Have you ever thought about Psalm 23 as "a political tract"? How does the similarity between Psalm 23 and Ezekiel 34 help?

---

2. Tamez, *Amnesty of Grace*, 134–40.

2. How would you describe a life of gratitude? Why is it so diffi-cult to live gratefully in the cultural context of North America (or the so-called developed world)?

3. Might Psalm 23 help us distinguish between wants and needs? And how would the ability to distinguish between wants and needs support a spirituality of justice-seeking and peacemaking?

4. Isaac Watts's metrical version of Psalm 23, "My Shepherd Will Supply My Need," concludes with the words, "Like a child at home." What does it mean to you to be "at home" with God?

5. Listen to Bobby McFerrin's version of Psalm 23 that is part of his collection, "Medicine Music" (available on YouTube, iTunes, and various music platforms). How does it help you hear Psalm 23 in a new way?

9

"Stop! And Know That I Am God!"

The City of God and the Peace of the World

THE FIRST PORTION OF the title of this chapter is a quotation from Psalm 46, a Song of Zion, and it is this category of psalm that we shall consider in this chapter. In a sense, these songs are songs of praise (see chapter 7), but the praise is directed to Jerusalem, which was known as God's city. As was the case with Psalm 23 (see chapter 8), it would appear at first sight that these psalms would have nothing to communicate to us about the pursuit of justice, righteousness, and peace. We might, for instance, pose the question: How could a very specific geographical location, Jerusalem, have anything to do with the peace of the world? As we pursue this question, we shall see that for the psalmists, Jerusalem had a revelatory capacity; what Jerusalem revealed was God's investment in and concern for the whole world. This is evident, first of all, in the location of two prominent Songs of Zion, Psalms 46 and 48.

Psalms 46–48: A Psalmic Triptych

The occurrence of two Songs of Zion, Psalms 46 and 48, surrounding Psalm 47, is almost certainly an intentional arrangement. In any case, the effect of this psalmic triptych is impressive. Although it is obviously not part of the enthronement collection (see chapter 2), Psalm 47 proclaims God's universal sovereignty. God is "a great king over all the earth" (v. 2; see vv. 7–8). So, "all you peoples" are invited to praise God (v. 1).

This invitation already implies what becomes explicit in v. 9—that is, the peoples and their leaders "gather as the people of the God of Abraham." In short, while Israel may have a special relationship with God (vv. 3–4), it is not an exclusive relationship; the other peoples and nations are claimed by God as well (see Ps 82:8). That Abraham is mentioned in v. 9 is not coincidental. The mention of nations and peoples in the context of God's claim on "all the earth" (vv. 2, 7) cannot help but recall Gen 12:1–3, where Abraham is promised a blessing, but not a blessing that involves the exclusion of others nor comes at the expense of others. Quite the contrary, Abraham and his descendants are to effect a blessing for nothing short of "all the families of the earth" (Gen 12:3; see also chapter 3, where it is noted that Gen 12:3 is also alluded to in Ps 72:17).

This larger canonical context is what prevents Psalm 47 from being simply imperialistic. Then, too, Psalm 47 itself strongly suggests that "the God of Abraham" wills the well-being of all the people of the world. Apparently, the gathering of world leaders is to turn in their "shields" (v. 9); that is, God wills that the world be disarmed so that all may experience the blessings of peace. At this point, Ps 47:9 has been anticipated by Ps 46:8–11, which also envisions the abolition of war as God "burns the shields with fire," thus making "wars cease to the end of the earth" (v. 9; see below on Psalm 46).

The fact that Psalm 47 is surrounded by Psalms 46 and 48 serves to make it eminently clear that Jerusalem, a specific geographical place, was understood to have world-encompassing significance. To contemplate Jerusalem (Psalm 46) or to visit Jerusalem (Psalm 48) was to be put in touch with the God of all peoples and nations, the God who wills the peace of the world.

Psalm 46

Actually, the universalistic perspective reinforced by the juxta-position of Psalms 46 and 47 is already evident in Psalm 46. To be sure, Jerusalem and its people have a special relationship with God. Jerusalem is "the city of God" (v. 4), and "God is in the midst of the city" (v. 5). God's presence is what promises pro-tection (vv. 7, 11), even amid cataclysmic natural circumstances (vv. 2–3) and international turmoil (v. 6; "shake" in v. 2 and "tot-ter" in v. 6 represent the same Hebrew word, thus linking the two threats to Jerusalem's security).

But beyond the special relationship that explains God's de-sire that Jerusalem be secure, it is also clear that God wants the world to be secure. Verses 8–10 are composed of four poetic lines in Hebrew, and three of these four lines end with the word "earth." The repetition is emphatic; God is at work in and on behalf of the whole earth! The "desolations" (v. 8) that God is bringing turn out to be a peace-making operation! What are desolated are various items of military hardware—bow, spear, shields—thus making "wars cease to the end of the earth" (v. 9).

It is in this context that we are invited to hear the familiar v. 10: "Be still, and know that I am God!" This invitation has usu-ally been heard as a call to slow down, relax, be quiet, meditate, and so on. In our hectic society, any of these things would be a good idea; but none of these things are what is called for here. In this context, "Be still" has the sense of "Stop it," "Throw down your weapons," or "Surrender." To contemplate Jerusalem is to be put in touch with the God who claims all "the nations" and "the earth" (v. 10), as Psalm 47 also makes clear. To know this God is to pursue peace on earth.

Given the concluding verses of Psalm 46, it is not surprising that elsewhere, too, Jerusalem is the starting point for the pursuit of peace on earth. In a crucial prophetic text, the importance of which is indicated by the fact that it occurs in both Isaiah and Micah, Jerusalem is the place that will host a meeting of "all the nations" (Isa 2:2; see "many nations" in Mic 4:2). The purpose of this meeting is to receive God's *torah*, "instruction" (Isa 2:3; Mic 4:2)—that is, to be put in touch with God's will (see chapter 4). And what is it? It starts with justice: God "will establish justice among the nations" (Isa 2:4, my translation; see Mic 4:3). And justice is the foundation for peace on a world-encompassing scale. The word *shalom* does not occur here, but the description of the outcome of this meeting says it all. There is nothing short of an amazing economic conversion—swords become plowshares and spears become pruning hooks. In other words, the resources of the military-industrial complex are converted into resources for agricultural production. So, not only will the people of the earth not "learn war any more" (Isa 2:4; Mic 4:3) but also everyone will be able to eat. As we saw earlier with Psalm 72 (see chapter 3), the *shalom* that God wills—"peace" or "comprehensive well-being"— begins with food (see also chapter 8). To contemplate Jerusalem, to visit Jerusalem, is to pursue justice for all. It is to move the world toward the peace that God wills—an end to warfare, an end to world hunger, and an end to every threat to human life and security. Psalm 48, which describes a visit to Jerusalem, will reinforce this conclusion.

Psalm 48

As in Psalm 46, the focus here is squarely upon Jerusalem, "the city of our God" (v. 1) and "the city of the great King" (v. 2). The psalmist's exuberance is evident in the poetic hyperbole with which Jerusalem is described—"beautiful in elevation . . . the joy of all the earth" (v. 2). The psalmist even imagines that the very sight of Jerusalem strikes panic in every would-be invader (vv. 4–7). Strictly speaking, of course, this was not the case; Jerusalem was destroyed in 587 BCE by the Babylonians. But we are dealing here with poetry, not historical reporting.

Unlike Psalm 46, Psalm 48 is not explicit about God's will to end all warfare. And unlike Isa 2:2–4 and Mic 4:1–3, Psalm 48 is not explicit about the divine will that all peoples of the world be able to eat. Psalm 48 does, however, celebrate the foundation upon which such comprehensive well-being depends—namely, God's *hesed*, "steadfast love" (v. 9), which "reaches to the ends of the earth" (v. 10; note that "name" in v. 10 connotes the divine character, the essence of which is "steadfast love," as indicated in Exod 34:6 and elsewhere). As in Pss 33:3 and 36:5–6 (see chapter 7), because God steadfastly loves the world, God wills righteousness and justice. Both are mentioned in Pss 48:10b–11, although the NRSV obscures their appearance. Verses 10b–11 form a lovely little chiasm that is evident in the following translation:

A Righteousness fills your right hand.
  B Let Mount Zion be glad,
  B' let the daughters of Judah rejoice,
A' because of your acts of justice. (my translation)

My translation has maintained the Hebrew word order, making it clear that the words "righteousness" (NRSV "victory") and "justice" (NRSV "judgments") encompass the celebration of God's will by Jerusalem and the towns (daughters) of Judah.

It is clear that the psalmist is not only contemplating Jerusalem but also locates him- or herself in the city—indeed, "in the midst of your temple" (v. 9). The visit to Jerusalem demonstrates the revelatory capacity of the city. In a powerful way, the psalmist has been put in touch with God's love, which in turn issues in a celebration of God's righteousness and justice, the foundation for peace. Not coincidentally, in this regard is the fact that the word *shalom* forms the final portion of the proper name, "Jeru*salem*," which probably should be understood as something like "gate of peace" or "foundation of peace."

It is this revelatory capacity of Jerusalem that explains why the psalmist sounds like a tour guide in vv. 12–13b:

Walk about Zion, go all around it,
  count its towers,
consider well its ramparts;
  go through its citadels. . . .

But the point is not that the visitor to Jerusalem be able to appreciate the architectural features of the city. Rather, the point is clear in the next lines that conclude the psalm:

> that you may tell the next generation
> > that this is God,
> our God forever and ever.
> > He will be our guide forever. (vv. 13c–14)

In short, Jerusalem is capable of putting visitors to the city in touch with God, thus preparing them to tell others. The connection between experiencing the city and telling future generations about God is even clearer in Hebrew, since the words "count" (v. 12) and "tell" (v. 13) translate the same Hebrew word. The English word "recount," instead of "tell," would better capture the connection. In any case, it is very clear that the city of Jerusalem itself has the capacity to reveal God and God's will—justice and righteousness, grounded in divine love (vv. 9–11). The divine will envisions and promises peace for Judah and Jerusalem, to be sure; but when Psalm 48 is heard following Psalms 46 and 47, it is clear that the divine will also envisions and promises peace for the whole world.

Psalm 87

One of the most remarkable of all the Psalms is a Song of Zion, Psalm 87. As in Psalms 46 and 48, God has a special relationship with Jerusalem. God "loves the gates of Zion" (v. 2), which is again addressed as the "city of God' (v. 3). But what is so striking is that the personified Jerusalem also claims a relationship with several of its traditional enemies—Rahab, which is Egypt (v. 4: see Isa 30:7); Babylon, which destroyed Jerusalem in 587 BCE (v. 4); and Philistia (v. 4; see Ps 60:8). God claims all these people and more, as if to say that everyone was born in Jerusalem (vv. 4–6). Jerusalem is everyone's spiritual home, regardless of nationality! The claim is remarkably simple but extraordinarily important—that is, every human being is a child of God! Such is the ultimate foundation for feeding every person and for pursuing the peace of the world.

The Songs of Zion for Today

The Songs of Zion may strike us contemporary readers as long-ago, far-away, and thus as quite irrelevant (despite the fact that Jerusalem is still very much a name in the news). Most people have never been and will never go to Jerusalem. But what Jerusalem represented in ancient times is still an experience that people of faith profess to have today—that is, an encounter with God.

Even in ancient times, especially after the destruction of Jerusalem in 587 BCE and the subsequent Babylonian exile and dispersion of Judeans throughout the Mediterranean world, there were Judeans (later Jews) who could never visit Jerusalem. Consequently, as Jerome Creach concludes, the Torah became a surrogate for the temple.[1] In other words, God could be met and God's will discerned by reading and hearing Scripture. So, in this somewhat simplified but largely accurate characterization, Judaism survived as a people of the book.

For Christianity, which eventually emerged out of Judaism, Jesus of Nazareth became the means of encountering God and being put in touch with God's will. So, Jesus could say, "Destroy this temple, and in three days I will raise it up" (John 2:19). The theology of the temple was transferred to Jesus; he became the locus of God's presence in the world, and he was the source of a new Torah (see Matt 5:1–2, where Jesus is portrayed as a new Moses).

In short, both Jews and Christians throughout the centuries have had the experience represented in the Songs of Zion—encountering God in a very specific place/person and thereby discerning God's will. To read and hear the Songs of Zion today is to be reminded that the God we encounter is the same God ancient Judeans encountered by way of visiting Jerusalem—that is, the God who loves the whole world, and who wills justice and righteousness toward the establishment of world-encompassing peace, including an end to warfare and an end to hunger. So, the Songs of Zion remain a spiritual resource for justice-seekers and peacemakers.

1. Creach, *Destiny of the Righteous*, 135–36.

Discussion Questions

1. How do the Songs of Zion contribute to an understanding that God works incarnationally (see chapters 3 and 10)?

2. Israel/Palestine is often called "the Holy Land," but how might the Songs of Zion suggest that every land is holy?

3. Certain denominations are typically known as "peace churches" (Quakers, Mennonites, etc.). Can there be a church that is not a "peace church"?

4. Psalm 46 is conceptually related to Isa 2:2–4, which features Jerusalem as a gathering place for all peoples and nations for the purpose of establishing justice and ending warfare. Isaiah 2:2–4 is inscribed on the stone wall in a spacious plaza across from the United Nations complex in Manhattan. How has the United Nations served as a peacemaking organization, and how might it continue to do so?

10

Hope for the World

The Psalms and Jesus

Reading *Christ* "Psalm-ologically"

OF ALL THE OLD Testament books, the book of Psalms is the most
frequently quoted or alluded to in the New Testament. It is very
clear, for instance, that the Gospel-writers could not tell the story
of Jesus, especially Jesus' suffering and death, without recourse to
the book of Psalms. The obvious similarity between Psalm 22 and
the passion narratives in the Gospels is prime evidence in this
regard. The similarity begins with the first line of Psalm 22, "My
God, my God, why have you forsaken me?" This line becomes
Jesus' words from the cross in the Gospels of Matthew and Mark
(Matt 27:46; Mark 15:34).

The fact that the Gospel-writers could not fully understand
Jesus nor tell the story of Jesus without recourse to the Psalms has
often led to the conclusion that the Psalms should be understood
as predictions of Jesus, and there is a long history of interpreting
the pray-er of the Psalms as Jesus himself. But there are other ways
to explain the similarity between Psalm 22 (and other psalms) and
the passion narratives and other portions of the New Testament—
for instance, as a first-century CE Jew, Jesus would have known

the Psalms, and the Gospel-writers may have borrowed from the Psalms to interpret Jesus' life and death. So, the traditional christological reading of the Psalms as predictive of Jesus or Jesus' voice is unnecessary; indeed, it can be quite problematic insofar as it ignores the set of life-experiences and contexts out of which the Psalms originated. The relationship between the Psalms and Jesus is undeniable and important, but instead of reading the Psalms christologically, I prefer to read Christ "psalm-ologically." In other words, I am interested in how the Psalms can help us understand what we mean when as Christians we say "Jesus *Christ*."

To my mind, this is so important, because most Christians seem to treat *Christ* as something like Jesus' last name; for them, it has no particular content or significance. But if we know and attend to the Psalms (as well as to other portions of the Old Testament), we realize that the term *Christ* has very rich and extraordinarily important content. It has everything to do with justice, righteousness, and peace. At this point, we return for a moment to chapter 3, concerning the royal psalms. Beginning with Psalm 2, the book of Psalms highlights the importance of the earthly king, who was known as God's "anointed" (Ps 2:2). The title, "anointed," is a translation of the Hebrew word traditionally transliterated as *messiah*, which came into Greek as *christos*. Psalm 2 also contains the phrase "my son" (Ps 2:7; every king was known as God's son). Psalm 72 very clearly describes the responsibility of the king—that is, the *christ*, the son of God—to be the establishment of justice, righteousness, and peace, defined as attendance to and provision for the poor, weak, and needy, beginning with feeding them.

This psalmic background is vitally important! It enables us to understand "psalm-ologically" the titles by which we name Jesus. In short, when we say Jesus *Christ*, and when we call Jesus the Son of God, we are inevitably talking about justice, righteousness, and peace. We are affirming that Jesus was a king who exercised royal power as God intends power to be exercised—not as self-aggrandizing force, but rather as loving servanthood that attends especially to the needs of the most vulnerable. Hence, from the Christian point of view, Jesus was not just another *messiah* or another son of God. Rather, he was *the Messiah* and *the* Son of God. But note well that proceeding "psalm-ologically" means that these titles have everything to do with justice, righteousness, and peace, as defined by Psalms 82 and 72, and reinforced by the other genres of psalms that we have examined.

Understanding *Christ* and Son of God "psalm-ologically" has further implications. For instance, it deepens our understanding of what we are actually praying for when we pray the Lord's Prayer. Consider the petition, "Your will be done, on earth as it is in heaven" (Matt 6:10). Recalling that the Psalms view the king as the earthly agent of God's will, and noting that it is King Jesus who is teaching his followers to pray this way, we realize that "Your will" has a very specific content—justice, righteousness, and peace. As we have seen repeatedly, these are the hallmarks of God's will or royal policy (see chapters 1–2, and note that the immediately preceding petition in the Lord's Prayer is "Your kingdom come"), and they were the responsibilities of the earthly king (see chapter 3). That King Jesus would teach his followers to pray for justice, righteousness, and peace is exactly what we would expect. As the fullest expression of human agency on God's behalf, Jesus exemplified God's will in a ministry of love and compassion that embraced and empowered the most vulnerable. In particular, it involved feeding them. Not coincidentally, in this regard, of course, it is crucial to note that the very next petition, which lies at the very heart of the Lord's Prayer, is, "Give us this day our daily bread" (Matt 6:11). From God's point of view, which Jesus fully embodied, justice, righteousness, and peace begin with providing food!

And speaking of food and feeding, to understand *Christ* "psalm-ologically" will serve to remind us that Communion, or the Lord's Supper, is actually meant to be understood and practiced as a meal. Jesus ate with his disciples and others. Jesus' command, "Do this in remembrance of me" (Luke 22:19), is an invitation to keep on eating together in such a way that everyone is fed, which is the way Jesus ate. That the Last Supper has become ritualized for Christian worship is fine, but it should not obscure the connection between liturgy and lifestyle—that is, the Lord's Supper should be seen as the Christian way of practicing (as in "Practice, practice, practice") what it means to eat graciously every day, sharing food so that all are fed. In so doing, Christians eat the way Jesus ate, and such is the appropriate way to remember him.

In other words, as the "body of Christ," the church is called to continue the work that Jesus did. As we reminded ourselves in the conclusion of chapter 3, Jesus did not do all the work that needs to be done in the world; there is still hunger, poverty, injustice, and oppression in many forms. But Jesus has empowered his body, by way of the Holy Spirit, to be the ongoing enfleshed logos in the world. This is an extraordinarily high calling, and given the ongoing injustice and oppression in the world, it is easy to be discouraged. Discouragement can take two forms. On the one hand, some folk give up entirely on God and God's purposes for the world, content to do the best they can for themselves and leave it at that. On the other hand, some folk relegate the pursuit and fulfillment of God's purposes to some future, otherworldly realm, which God alone will enact. In both cases, there is an abandonment of human agency. It is asserted that we human beings have nothing to do with the establishment of justice, righteousness, and peace that God wills for the world. In other words, the claim is that God's Spirit cannot work in and through us.

These two forms of discouragement and the consequent abandonment of human agency represent the antithesis of the definition of spirituality that I have proposed (see the introduction):

> Spirituality is the work of God the Holy Spirit *in our lives* . . . *calling us* to the service of God's righteousness in the world.

Notice especially the words *our* and *us*! God's work in the world will not be achieved by God alone nor by us alone, but rather *by God and us together*. As we suggested in the concluding section of chapter 2, this is the way that God has chosen to work in the world. The reason is simple: God is love, and love requires human freedom in order for genuine relationship (that is, love) to be possible. But, as we said as well, this is God's "great risk." Clearly, we human beings have not responded and do not respond faithfully in the pursuit of God's will for the world. That's the bad news. But the good news is that God, who is gracious and merciful, continues to love us, continues to love the world, and continues to call "us to the service of God's righteousness in the world."

Waiting for God and Hope for the World

What all this means is that spirituality, as we have defined it and as the Psalms help us to understand it, will always be character-ized by what the Psalms call "waiting"—or, to use a word that perhaps sounds more familiar, hope. Two very familiar psalms conclude by featuring waiting:

> Wait for the LORD;
> > be strong and let your heart take courage;
> wait for the LORD! (Ps 27:14)

> Be strong, and let your heart take courage,
> > all you who wait for the LORD. (Ps 31:24)

Psalms 27 and 31 capture what will be the perennial posture of the people of God—waiting, or hope. Because of God's commitment to partner with us human beings—in other words, because God loves unfailingly—we shall always be living toward the fulfillment of God's will for the world.

But some Christians will object that Jesus is coming back someday to complete the fulfillment of God's will for justice, righteousness, and peace. So bringing about justice in the world is not our responsibility. However, for those who are expecting, waiting for, and hoping for Jesus to return, their waiting should not be passive, because Jesus called and calls his followers to actively enter God's realm and to do God's will (see Mark 1:14–15). As we have seen in the Psalms, human agency is of the essence (see chap-ter 3). In the final analysis, to read Christ "psalm-ologically" will mean that the people of God will be motivated and energized to resist injustice, oppression, and dehumanization as they work to move the world toward the justice, righteousness, and peace that God wills.

To be sure, even if the fullness of God's kingdom justice lies in the future, the New Testament leads its readers to expect that it can and should be anticipated in the present. The kingdom is among us. This is nowhere clearer than in the Gospel of John, which is the latest of the Gospels and which anchors the four-Gospel collection. John emphasizes that eternal life is a present reality in the Spirit, which Jesus breathed on his disciples (John 20:22), thus empowering them and the later church to be the ongoing "enfleshed logos" in the world.[1] The future is NOW, says John over and over in numerous different ways, even as he acknowledges that its fullness is still to come (5:24–30). Empowered by the Holy Spirit, and following the lead of Jesus, the church continues "the service of God's righteousness in the world."

At this point, as is the case at other points as well, the Psalms cohere with the prophets (see chapters 7 and 9). Although she is commenting on the prophetic book of Habakkuk and the prophet's call to "wait" (Hab 2:3) for the divine response to current injustice (Hab 1:4), what Ofelia Ortega says about hope applies also to the Psalms as well:

> What makes the prophet's message about the future so brilliant is precisely this: That in all the texts, directly or indirectly, there is an appeal to conversion and change. . . . Not waiting, not dreaming of a better tomorrow, is one of the worst forms of incredulity. . . . It is true that there were prophecies that were never accomplished, but it is not because the prophets were mistaken. No, simply because we did not act as "history watchers" [see Hab 2:1], men and women of the coming tomorrow. That's why reading Habakkuk calls us desperately to keep hope.[2]

As was suggested in the concluding sections of chapters 2 and 3, the persistence of injustice and oppression is not God's will, nor

1. Scroggs, *Christology in Paul and John*, 85, 88.
2. Ortega, "Revolutionary Hope," 127.

is it an indication of God's absence or failure to act. Rather, it is an indication of *our* failure to act. The persistence of injustice and oppression is discouraging, but it need not be a source of despair. Rather, when we read *Christ* "psalm-ologically," we hear both Jesus and the Psalms calling "us desperately to keep hope," to "wait for the LORD" (Ps 27:14).

An eloquent example of being inspired and energized by hope to confront and address the injustice and suffering of the world is Scott Harrison, the founder and CEO of *charity:water*, which has carried out over 28,000 water projects that have allowed 8.5 million people to have clean, healthy water. Harrison came to realize, in essence, that waiting or hope is the perennial posture of the faithful because our work is never done. As he puts it:

> There's an old rabbinic saying that I love: "Do not be afraid of work that has no end." That's how I've come to see this journey [of providing clean water to the human community]. If your work is in the service of others—if you are compassionately pursuing an end to the suffering of people less fortunate than you—then your work will simply never end. The idea of endless work used to scare me. But not anymore.

Harrison concludes his book entitled *Thirst* by pointing out that we have a "deficit of hope" nowadays. He cites Pope Francis and his observation that "a single individual is enough for hope to exist."[3] In short, hope energizes us to do "work that has no end." Waiting for God will always be the posture of the faithful. As William Sloane Coffin once put it: "Hope criticizes what is, hopelessness rationalizes it. Hope resists, hopelessness adapts."[4] To read *Christ* "psalm-ologically" is to be inspired and energized to resist injustice, oppression, and dehumanization. It is to be open to God's Spirit calling us to and equipping us for "work that has no end"—the pursuit of the justice, righteousness, and peace that God wills for the world. Such is the essence of spirituality.

---

3. Harrison, *Thirst*, 312–13.
4. Coffin, *Passion for the Possible*, 88.

Discussion Questions

1. Various forms of so-called "Christian Nationalism" have become prominent in recent years in the US as well as other nations. How does understanding Jesus "psalm-ologically" counter the claim that God favors the US or any other particular country?

2. What do you think about when you pray, "Your will be done, on earth as it is in heaven"?

3. How does understanding Jesus "psalm-ologically" impel us to end world hunger?

4. Consider that Mark 14:7, "For you always have the poor with you," has often been cited as an excuse for apathy when it comes to addressing poverty, despite the fact that Deut 15:11 (on which Mark 14:7 is based) understands poverty as an invitation to generosity. In any case, how can understanding Jesus "psalm-ologically" be understood as an invitation to end poverty and hunger—in essence, an invitation "to work that has no end"?

11

Conclusion

IN CONCLUSION, WE RETURN briefly to where we began—that is,
with the psalmist's affirmation in Ps 120:7, "I am for peace." As
suggested in the introduction, this affirmation can be seen as a
summary statement of the spirituality derived from the book of
Psalms. Why? As we have seen, beginning with Psalm 82, a key
part of what constitutes divinity or god-ness is the unwavering
commitment to justice, which is the keyword in Psalm 82, defined
very clearly as attentiveness to and provision of the most vulnerable. Psalm 82 also features righteousness, and as Psalms 96 and
98 assert, God has come into the world to "establish justice in the
world with righteousness" (Pss 96:13; 98:9). From Psalm 72, we
learn that this mission of justice and righteousness aims at the
establishment of *shalom*, "peace" or "comprehensive well-being."
It was a mission that in ancient times was entrusted to the earthly
king, but it became a mission entrusted to the whole people of
God. As we have also seen, a variety of types of psalms are related
to this mission.

Our God-centered approach to spirituality means that it is
crucial to discern what is God's will and work. The Psalms make it
clear—justice, righteousness, and *shalom*. And because spirituality involves God's "calling us to the service of God's righteousness

in the world," we can properly conclude that a spirituality derived from the Psalms amounts fundamentally to joining God at God's work in the world. A good place to begin, therefore, is with the psalmist's affirmation, "I am for peace," followed of course by the exercise of our human agency in the pursuit of the justice, righteousness, and peace that God wills.

We conclude with one final reminder of the connection between justice and peace, involving the specific context of the psalmist's affirmation, "I am for peace." Psalm 120 is the first psalm in a collection, the Songs of Ascents, which were likely used in conjunction with pilgrimages to Jerusalem. Not coincidentally in this regard, Psalm 120 locates the psalmist outside the land (see v. 5); Psalm 121 involves a journey; and Psalm 122 locates the psalmist(s) in Jerusalem: "Our feet are standing within your gates, O Jerusalem" (Ps 122:2). By virtue of the three-fold repetition in vv. 6–8, the keyword in Psalm 122 is clearly *shalom*:

> Pray for the peace of Jerusalem . . .
> Peace be within your walls . . .
> I will say, "Peace be within you."

Earlier in Psalm 122, we hear that the purpose of the pilgrimage to Jerusalem is "to give thanks to the name of the LORD" (v. 4). And in the very next verse, which lies at the heart of the psalm, we see that gratitude is due to God on account of God's provision for the establishment of justice:

> For there the thrones for justice were set up,
> the thrones of the house of David. (my translation)

As suggested in chapter 9, Jerusalem had a revelatory capacity, and what is revealed in Psalm 122 is God's commitment to peace, grounded in justice. Psalm 122 is a Song of Zion, and as Psalm 46—another Song of Zion—makes clear (see chapter 9), the peace desired for Jerusalem is ultimately to extend to peace on earth (see also Isa 2:2–4; Mic 4:1–3).

To put it in very simple terms, sometimes bumper-sticker slogans and protest-signs are correct:

If you want peace, work for justice.

No justice, no peace.

Know justice, know peace.

Or, as the psalmist put it simply, "I am for peace." For the Book of Psalms, spirituality begins here!

Discussion Questions

1. Use Ps 120:7, "I am for peace," as your opening line, and write a short credo or poem about what you understand justice-seeking and peacemaking to mean and to involve. In short, how will you aim to seek justice and peace in your own life, in your community, in your nation, and in the world?

2. How have the Psalms helped you to reach this understanding?

Bibliography

Boff, Leonardo. *Cry of the Earth, Cry of the Poor.* Translated by Phillip Berryman. Maryknoll, NY: Orbis, 1997.

Borg, Marcus. *Meeting Jesus Again for the First Time: The Historical Jesus and the Heart of Contemporary Faith.* San Francisco: HarperOne, 1995.

Brueggemann, Walter. "The Costly Loss of Lament." *Journal for the Study of the Old Testament* 36 (1986) 57–71.

———. *The Message of the Psalms: A Theological Commentary.* Minneapolis: Fortress, 1985.

Calvin, John. *Commentary on the Book of Psalms.* Vol. 1. Edinburgh: Calvin Translation Society, 1845.

Cardenal, Ernesto. *Psalms.* New York: Crossroad, 1981.

Coffin, William Sloane. *A Passion for the Possible: A Message to US Churches.* 2nd ed. Louisville, KY: Westminster John Knox, 2004.

Colligan, Richard Bruxvoort. "I Am For Peace (Psalm 120)." In a CD collection entitled *Psalms of Justice and Longing.* Worldmaking.net (ASCAP), 2014.

Conrad, Edgar W. *Reading Isaiah.* Overtures in Biblical Theology. Minneapolis: Fortress, 1991.

Creach, Jerome F. D. *The Destiny of the Righteous in the Psalms.* St. Louis, MO: Chalice, 2008.

Crossan, John Dominic. *The Birth of Christianity: Discovering What Happened in the Years Immediately after the Execution of Jesus.* San Francisco: HarperOne, 1998.

Davis, Ellen F. *Opening Israel's Scriptures.* Oxford: Oxford University Press, 2019.

———. *Scripture, Culture, and Agriculture: An Agrarian Reading of the Bible.* Cambridge: Cambridge University Press, 2009.

Eden Theological Seminary Faculty. *Spirituality: The Work of God the Holy Spirit in Our Lives.* St. Louis, MO: Eden Theological Seminary, 1990.

Endres, John C., SJ. "Psalms and Spirituality in the 21st Century." *Interpretation* 56 (2002) 143–54.

Firth, David G. *Surrendering Retribution in the Psalms: Responses to Violence in Individual Complaints.* Paternoster Biblical Monographs. Reprint, Eugene, OR: Wipf and Stock, 2006.

Francis, Leah Gunning. *Faith after Ferguson: Resilient Leadership in Pursuit of Racial Justice.* St. Louis, MO: Chalice, 2021.

———. *Ferguson and Faith: Sparking Leadership and Awakening Community.* St. Louis, MO: Chalice, 2015.

Francis, Pope. *Laudato Si': On Care for Our Common Home.* Vatican City: Libreria Editrice Vaticana, 2015.

Goldingay, John. *Psalms 42–89.* Vol. 2 of *Psalms.* Baker Commentary on the Old Testament Wisdom and Psalms. Grand Rapids: Baker Academic, 2007.

Hall, Douglas John. *God and Human Suffering: An Exercise in the Theology of the Cross.* Minneapolis: Augsburg, 1986.

Harrison, Scott. *Thirst: A Story of Redemption, Compassion, and a Mission to Bring Clean Water to the World.* New York: Currency, 2018.

Jenkins, Philip. "Liberating Word: The Power of the Bible in the Global South." *The Christian Century*, July 11, 2006, 22–26.

Levenson, Jon. "The Sources of Torah: Psalm 119 and the Modes of Revelation in Second Temple Judaism." In *Ancient Israelite Religion*, edited by P. D. Miller Jr. et al., 559–74. Philadelphia: Fortress, 1987.

Luther, Martin. "Preface to the Psalter." In vol. 35 of *Luther's Works*, edited by E. Theodore Bachmann, 253–57. Philadelphia: Fortress, 1960.

Martin, Chad. "In the Lectionary, July 2, 13th Sunday in Ordinary Time: Psalm 13." *The Christian Century*, July 2023, 24.

Mays, James L. *The Lord Reigns: A Theological Handbook to the Psalms.* Louisville, KY: Westminster John Knox, 1994.

———. *Preaching and Teaching the Psalms.* Edited by P. D. Miller and G. M. Tucker. Louisville, KY: Westminster John Knox, 2006.

———. "Psalm 13." *Interpretation* 34 (1980) 279–83.

———. *Psalms.* Interpretation. Louisville, KY: John Knox, 1994.

McCann, J. Clinton, Jr. "The Hope of the Poor: The Psalms in Worship and Our Search for Justice." In *Touching the Altar: The Old Testament for Christian Worship*, edited by Carol M. Bechtel, 155–78. Grand Rapids: Eerdmans, 2008.

———. "The Single Most Important Text in the Entire Bible: Toward a Theology of the Psalms." In *Soundings in the Theology of Psalms: Perspectives and Methods in Contemporary Scholarship*, edited by Rolf A. Jacobson, 63–75. Minneapolis: Fortress, 2011.

McKibben, Bill. *The Comforting Whirlwind: God, Job, and the Scale of Creation.* Cambridge, MA: Cowley, 2005.

Mongé-Greer, Erica. *Divine Council, Ethics, and Resistance in Psalm 82.* Eugene, OR: Pickwick, 2023.

Ortega, Ofelia. "Revolutionary Hope in the Church after Christendom." In *Hope for the World: Mission in a Global Context*, edited by Walter Brueggemann, 115–36. Louisville, KY: Westminster John Knox, 2001.

Peterson, Eugene H. *The Message: The New Testament, Psalms, and Proverbs in Contemporary Language*. Colorado Springs, CO: Nav, 1995.

Pipher, Mary. *The Shelter of Each Other: Rebuilding Our Families*. New York: Ballantine, 1996.

Pleins, J. David. *The Psalms: Songs of Tragedy, Hope, and Justice*. Maryknoll, NY: Orbis, 1993.

"Quotes about Hunger." https://www.hungerhile.org.

Scroggs, Robin. *Christology in Paul and John*. Proclamation Commentaries. Philadelphia: Fortress, 1988.

Tamez, Elsa. *The Amnesty of Grace: Justification by Faith from a Latin American Perspective*. Translated by Sharon H. Ringe. Nashville: Abingdon, 1993.

Unruh, Anita M., et al. "Spirituality Unplugged: A Review of Commonalities and Contentions, and a Resolution." *Canadian Journal of Occupational Therapy* 69 (2002) 5–19.

Walker-Jones, Arthur. *The Green Psalter: Resources for an Ecological Spirituality*. Minneapolis: Fortress, 2009.

Westermann, Claus. *Praise and Lament in the Psalms*. Translated by Keith R. Crim and Richard N. Soulen. Atlanta: John Knox, 1981.

Westermeyer, Paul. *Let Justice Sing: Hymnody and Justice*. American Essays in Liturgy. Collegeville, MN: Liturgical, 1998.

Wilson, Gerald H. *The Editing of the Hebrew Psalter*. Society of Biblical Literature Dissertation Series. Chico, CA: Scholars, 1985.

———. "The Use of Royal Psalms at the 'Seams' of the Hebrew Psalter." *Journal for the Study of the Old Testament* 35 (1986) 85–94.

Zenger, Erich. *A God of Vengeance? Understanding the Psalms of Divine Wrath*. Translated by Linda M. Maloney. Louisville, KY: Westminster John Knox, 1996.